EDITH WHARTON

In the same series:

    (continued on page 119)

MODERN LITERATURE MONOGRAPHS
GENERAL EDITOR: Lina Mainiero

EDITH WHARTON

Richard H. Lawson

FREDERICK UNGAR PUBLISHING CO.
NEW YORK

1977

Copyright © 1977 by Frederick Ungar Publishing Co., Inc.
Printed in the United States of America
Design by Anita Duncan

Library of Congress Cataloging in Publication Data

Lawson, Richard H
    Edith Wharton.

    (Modern literature monographs)
    Bibliography: p.
    Includes index.
    1. Wharton, Edith Newbold Jones, 1862-1937—Criticism
and interpretation.
PS3545.H16Z692   813'.5'2   77-40
ISBN 0-8044-2496-9

Contents

Chronology

I

Life in Society

Edith Newbold Jones, later to become Edith Wharton, was born during the Civil War—in 1862—into a New York society that had not yet been subjected to conquest and absorption by the millionaires of that war. That postwar social change is a topic that was to comprise the stuff of some of her best novels. Her parents, George Frederic and Lucretia Rhinelander Jones, belonged to the society that had dominated New York from the Dutch and English colonial era until, say, 1870 or 1880.

Edith reminded us more than once—she may have been protesting too much—that we are not to regard the members of this social group as a hereditary aristocracy, that they had been and remained a bourgeoisie. But they were a bourgeoisie who had through the centuries grown rich from the greatly increased value of Manhattan real estate, who disdained participation in both commerce and politics, who were oriented more toward Europe than toward the continent to their west, who pursued art and culture but ostracized any contemporary artists in their midst, and who, finally, produced an inbred—both genetically and socially—society which lived according to a highly formalized code.

George and Lucretia Jones were not ambitious if measured by the standards of today's striving society. They lived well in New York and in Europe when times were good; they trimmed their financial sails, in New York and Europe, when times were bad. They followed the dictates of fashion.

Edith's father had a library of six or seven hundred volumes: English dramatists, including Shakespeare; French dramatists; novelists and poets beginning with Plutarch, Milton, Pope, Swift, Sterne, Defoe, Scott, Irving, Thackeray, and Longfellow, among others. Despite this wealth of available material, Edith's father and mother did not read much. Her father perhaps looked sporadically into one or another of his books; her mother's favorite reading consisted of current popular novels. Despite their lack of interest in literature, Edith's parents were heirs to a tradition that included a "feeling for good English." This, along with (occasionally restricted) access to good books, was handed down to their daughter Edith. As an adult, Edith, who was conspicuously estranged from her mother, evinced a unique gratitude to her for her insistence on good English—not necessarily bookish, but not slangy either.

Edith never attended school. Daughters of houses like that of the Joneses were educated by governesses for their ultimate role in their society—that of wives with the proper social graces. This kind of education, however, was not necessarily limited. It could, and in Edith's case it did, produce a girl of almost frightening erudition. She learned French, German, and Italian before she was nine. By the time she was in her early teens she was reading Goethe, Balzac, even medieval German and French poets. She had at least browsed through everything in her father's library—it was not her habit to read every book she picked up from beginning to end. Family friends gave her books, for she was beginning to attract attention as the girl who read avidly—which was definitely not what the Joneses had had in mind in making available to her the varied, sometimes highly developed talents of a series of governesses. If she continued in this direction, Edith would never become adept at the social game that was the proper destiny of young ladies of her family and social background.

The Joneses were now in New York, now in Paris, Cannes, Florence, the Black Forest, Madrid, and Newport in season. In the latter resort, New York society was beginning to erect great and splendid homes to repair to when summer drove them out of New York City. Here too the social rituals were practiced with undiminished rigor. Edith did not especially resist them. That would have been unthinkable even for a forceful daughter, and Edith was shy and introverted. In her teens, when the social advantage of beauty could not have escaped her perception, she possessed no more than average looks. She was not without friends, with whom she shared a love for literature, but her mother may well have foreseen that getting her properly married at an early age was not going to be easy.

Edith's taste for reading, in any case, contributed to the foreshortening of her already rather adult-like childhood by one year. Her mother decreed that she was to come out, that is, enter society, at seventeen rather than the customary eighteen. Edith seems to have welcomed the prospect of being officially regarded as an adult. At her coming-out party (which, as arranged by her mother, was not as splendid as it might have been), she was, however, overcome by shyness to the point of refusing to dance even with the friends of her brother Harry.

Harry was her favorite. With her oldest brother Freddy she was less close. Both boys were much older than Edith; they were already in their teens when she was born. Very much the baby of the family, in her early childhood she was indulged and protected by the male members, even if there was a distinct lack of maternal sympathy.

Her first attempt to write a novel was at the age of eleven. For the purpose, her mother gave her some used wrapping paper. As if this sort of writing material were not discouragement enough, her mother's icy criticism of her first few lines served to still Edith's creative enthusiasm for the time being. In her opening lines, Edith had been so

imperceptive of her society's standards as to imply that
drawing rooms could be other than tidy! This episode Edith
recounts in her autobiography, *A Backward Glance*.

Edith does not, however, mention her first published
work, when she was about thirteen. She had become acquainted with Emelyn Washburn, the daughter of the rector
of Calvary Church, and six years Edith's senior. The two
enthusiastically studied German together. They sold to a
magazine some translations of German poetry, which were
largely Edith's work. Emelyn Washburn also seems to have
played a role in persuading Edith's mother to remove
Goethe's works from the category of forbidden books.

Around 1871 or 1872, Anna Bahlmann entered Edith's
life as governess and teacher, and stayed to become confidante, secretary, literary associate, and lifelong friend. In
1880, Anna Bahlmann accompanied the Joneses on what
was to be their last family trip to Europe. The trip was in the
first place a response to medical advice that Mr. Jones's life
might be prolonged in the warmer climate of southern
France. Another reason for the trip was to try to separate
her from a suitor named Harry Stevens. (She was getting
about, and once secure in a circle of friends, she was losing
at least some of her shyness.) Finally, Edith herself had
been wanting to return to Europe—a desire that was pro-
phetic of her later long residence there. After two years
abroad her father died. His death was a severe loss for
Edith, for she had had a loving relationship with him that
was not paralleled in her relationship with her mother.

Back in New York, and in mourning, Edith was ap-
proaching the age of twenty, still unmarried. By this time,
1882, the static society into which she had been born was
clearly changing. The new millionaires, the Astors and the
Vanderbilts, much given to vulgar public display of wealth,
were making their way into the formerly closed circle of
New York society. The resulting composite society, now
generally characterized by the unseemly manners of the

parvenus, was not regarded with approval by the widowed Lucretia Jones or by Edith.

The ineffective resistance of the older society to the parvenus, the uneasy mixing of the two societies, and the final triumph of what Edith called the Invaders (who now boasted an admixture of respectability, obtained either through intermarriage or purchase) is the material of all of her best novels except *Ethan Frome*. The resistance, the mixing, and the surrender are at the root of the social attitudes she depicted or implied in these novels. Coming of age in a rapidly changing society, she was never able to make peace with the emergent society. She despised its vulgar presuppositions, including, above all, its materialism, which did not mean that she approved of the manners—the rigid external forms—of the society in which she grew up. She perceived the excessive devotion to such manners as a futile self-protective device in a society that was already doomed.

In 1885, when she was twenty-three, nearing the age when unmarried young ladies of her class were considered spinsters, Edith married Edward "Teddy" Wharton, of proper family and twelve years her senior. Teddy Wharton's was apparently the first viable offer of marriage that Edith received, although she seems to have been in love at least twice previously with young men nearer her own age.

The first romance was with Harry Stevens, who followed Edith to Europe in 1880 or 1881 and pursued his courtship there. Young Stevens succeeded in reducing the opposition of Edith's parents, and when they returned to Newport, Edith's widowed mother consented to an engagement. What Harry Stevens could not reduce, unfortunately, was the opposition of *his* widowed, parvenu mother, who was apparently loath to loosen her grip on her son's trust fund of a million and a quarter. The engagement was broken.

Edith's next young man was Walter van Rensselaer Berry. While, to her despair at the time, their romance did not lead to an engagement, it did lead to a lifelong friend-

ship, and among the facets of that friendship was a considerable influence by Berry on Edith's writing. She first met
Berry in the summer of 1883 at Bar Harbor, Maine, which
was a less citified resort than Newport had become by then.
Berry's family was old New York, like Edith's, and there
hardly could have been any objection to a match by either
family. Berry, however, failed to propose marriage, to Edith
then or later—or to any woman ever.

A lawyer, inclined toward international law, in which
he ultimately enjoyed a most successful career, Berry also
was a cultivated and discerning admirer of literature. We
can imagine Edith's joyful responsiveness to a social equal
who like her was interested in literature. Their relationship
quickly advanced to a serious stage—but the word was not
spoken. Berry departed, for Washington, D. C. At least,
Edith's humiliation was private this time, in contrast to that
connected with the broken engagement to Harry Stevens. It
was fourteen years before she and Berry were to see each
other again in any significant way.

The newly-married Teddy and Edith Wharton gave
themselves over to the New York and Newport social ritual.
Edith did not complain; what we may think was her innate
distaste for this kind of life was perhaps compensated for by
her delight in leaving her mother's roof, and even more by
frequent travel by private yacht to the Caribbean. There was
even an unforgettably delightful cruise through the Aegean
islands in 1888. She seems at any rate to have been content
for a while in her role as wife. Within a few years, however,
the marriage became unhappy; it is likely, indeed, that the
apparent early contentment was more superficial than real.
It seems rather clear that her turning to writing in the late
1880s—sporadically at first—was related to a growing marital disenchantment. The frequent assertion, however, that
writing was prescribed as therapy for her own nervous
condition—she suffered psychic breakdowns in 1894 and
1898—is quite false.

Teddy Wharton, wealthy in his own right, was representative of the men in his and Edith's society. He had no real profession; he was a dilettante hunter, a good fly-fisherman. Moreover, he was a generally ineffective person. Meanwhile, Edith became outwardly less and less like the shy girl in her teens. She acted more decisively and more forcefully. She was establishing some reputation as a successful writer of fiction (short stories, novellas, and a full-length historical novel) as well as a translator of German. She was avid in her pursuit and enjoyment of learning. (Walter Berry had claimed—he was probably rationalizing his own reticence to some extent—that her relentless intellectuality was a bar to courting.) Teddy Wharton was in effect reduced to either trailing around after her or to living separately from her, which happened more and more after a few joint winters in Paris.

The strained relationship could only get worse when Teddy began exhibiting symptoms of mental ill health. There were periods of apparent recovery, accompanied by reconciliation, but his manic-depressive condition became increasingly severe. Edith seems to have been patient, even sometimes hopeful, but in the long run it was to no avail. Finally, in 1912, after several vain attempts at persuasion, she talked him into entering a Swiss sanitarium. In 1913 she divorced Teddy Wharton. There were no children of this marriage, and there is no direct indication, either in her letters or in her best-known fiction, that she regarded this as a deprivation. In her post-1920 fiction it is, however, possible to perceive some such indication of regret.

Walter Berry reentered Edith's life in 1897, when he was a summer guest at Land's End, the Whartons' summer home at Newport. Edith had collaborated with her architect-friend Ogden Codman, who had advised on the restoration of Land's End, on a book to be called *The Decoration of Houses*. The book had already been accepted—with scant enthusiasm, to be sure—by Scribner's. Edith was rewriting the rather clumsy first draft under pressure of an imminent deadline. Berry took the matter in hand and suggested not only substantial changes in style, but a basic reorganization of the material. Under his friendly supervision, Edith accomplished the rewriting. From *The Decoration of Houses*, which, contrary to all expectations, enjoyed a long, steady success, Edith gained the first royalty check of her life.

In the following year, as Edith was recovering from a nervous breakdown, Berry continued to function as her literary adviser. He encouraged her with her short stories, praising her style and sympathetically suggesting improvements here and there. As before, and subsequently, Berry's domain of helpfulness was primarily style. Edith seems to have accepted such help gratefully, even as she, along with Teddy, had long accepted his friendship. For many years Berry was a frequent and welcome guest of the Whartons, first in the United States, then more and more in Europe.

After Edith's divorce from Teddy, many of her friends thought Berry would now ask her to marry him. But there seems never to have been a real likelihood of this, and most likely Edith did not expect it. Berry enjoyed the company of women, many of whom, by the way, were very far from being Edith's intellectual equals, but all his life long he carefully avoided the sort of proximity that might have led to marriage. The mutually rewarding friendship with Edith continued until Berry's death in Paris in 1927, but neither early nor late were they lovers.

Edith's only lover, it would appear, was Morton Fullerton, an American journalist, Paris correspondent of the London *Times*, and a friend and admirer of Henry James. Fullerton entered her life in Paris in 1907. Later that same year he visited the Whartons at The Mount, the large and luxurious country home that the Whartons had had built near Lenox, Massachusetts, after Newport and Land's End had become intolerable to Edith. At The Mount, in the designing and building of which Edith had played a primary role, she now was playing hostess, in season and between Paris seasons, to a never-ending and ever-changing group of friends, fellow artists, and congenial professional people. Fullerton was among them.

He and Edith became lovers the next year, in Paris. The intimate relationship lasted somewhat longer than a year and was obviously much more deeply felt on Edith's part than on his. Given the highly moral tenets inculcated in Edith by family and society, her intense passion was accompanied by an intense feeling of guilt, not lessened by her subsequent charge, in her divorce complaint, of adulterous episodes on Teddy's part. The principal literary reflections of Edith's passion were in her journal and in some extraordinary poetry. The latter was not at all daring in form but quite definitely so in content, especially for the writer of novels, which, far from being erotically specific, are masterpieces of the allusive. In this connection it is worth noting that even while Edith's tempestuous affair with Fullerton was introducing her, at the age of forty-five, to emotions and passions she had never known (her marriage to Teddy was practically sexless), she continued to present to the world a picture of discreet detachment and self-containment.

When Edith was still in her twenties, mutual friends of her and Henry James twice made attempts to get the two acquainted with each other. Neither attempt was successful. On the first, Edith recalled, she staked everything on looking pretty and wearing a pretty dress to a party. The Master paid no attention to her and she was too tongue-tied in his presence to push herself forward. On the second occasion a beautiful new hat proved an equally ineffective lure.

It was almost ten years after the second nonmeeting that Edith sent him a story and James thereupon became aware of her writing, which he characterized then, in 1899, as that of an almost too susceptible student of his. This observation must have been the beginning of the extremely durable misapprehension that Edith was and remained always very much under the literary influence of James. James also observed, and it was not the last time, that she should make old New York, the world she knew best, the subject of her fiction. This bit of advice Edith did not feel compelled to accept in any thoroughgoing way.

Her first personal meeting with James did not occur until the winter of 1903. It was in response to James's open-ended invitation, extended along with his comments on the story. A very close personal and literary friendship resulted, which ended only with James's death.

James and the Whartons took to visiting back and forth quite regularly in the United States, in England, and in France. Edith was initiated into the Jamesian circle in England, James was introduced to Edith's widening circle of French artist-friends. James was persuaded to tour a good bit of rural France with the Whartons—who were among the very first owners and regular users of that recent invention, the automobile. James is on record as dreading Edith's sweeping him away on one auto trip or another, but in fact he consistently enjoyed himself in her company. His expressions of disapproval were not confined to auto trips. He noted bittersweetly, for example, the vast difference in the amounts of money their respective literary endeavors were bringing in. Edith, within a few years of her first meeting with James, was indeed making very good money. She always managed, however, to spend as much as she earned, though by no means exclusively on herself. (Her inherited income did, of course, provide a financial cushion.)

There may have been a grain of truth in the (perhaps slightly jealous) assertions of James's friends that Edith was thoughtless in frequently disturbing James's work routine. Certainly she would brook no parallel interference in her own routine. Each morning she worked in bed on a writing board for perhaps three or four hours, whether or not she had guests—and she usually did. A bit after twelve o'clock she would descend to her guests and assume her almost equally beloved role of genial hostess and conversationalist. In the last-named capacity she was as much at ease in French or Italian as in English. Through the years she talked more and more in French. In fact French became so natural to her that in her later writing she occasionally encountered difficulties related to her increasing separation from her native language.

By the time Edith divorced Teddy, in 1913, Paris was her home. In it, or near it—with winters in another home on the French Riviera—she lived for another twenty-four years, sallying forth for European and African travels with a zest hardly daunted by increasing age. She returned twice to the United States—for a few days each time—and was appalled at how rapidly materialism had advanced. She turned out novels at regular intervals. The later ones, especially those published in the 1920s, are inferior when evaluated against her earlier works. Perhaps the separation, so long and so sustained, from the American sources of her fiction, contributed to the failure of verisimilitude so evident in most of these later works. Quite likely the requirements of the slick magazines, principally *The Pictorial Review* and *The Delineator*, for which she was now writing, with their focus on the mass market and the selling of advertising space, also contributed to this failure.

From time to time Edith objected to her new editors' requirements; she was not, she averred at one point, in the business of selling "prose by the yard." (Nonetheless, her income from writing now rose to new peaks.) It was all somewhat paradoxical. Her name and reputation attracted advertisers and readers; but they were readers in whom she could have had little cultural confidence and to whom she was in effect required to write down. After *The Age of Innocence* she wrote ten undistinguished novels, which first appeared serially in magazines and subsequently in book form under the Appleton imprint. Perhaps only *The Mother's Recompense* rises a bit above the level of mediocrity.

But whatever the critics said, and it was increasingly unkind, Edith apparently knew what she was doing artistically. For the failure of verisimilitude, the shallow characterizations, the formula plots, and the stereotyped, somehow not quite authentic language turned out not to be permanent afflictions, but merely her adaptation to the requirements of her new medium. The superior quality of Edith's last, uncompleted, posthumous novel, *The Buccaneers*, which harks back to her own New York generation of the 1870s, suggests that her powers had not really deserted her during her magazine-fiction era, but had merely lain idle.

Edith Wharton, in striking contrast to contemporary writers, had remarkably little to say for public consumption about herself as a person or as a writer. That little, chiefly as revealed in *A Backward Glance*, published in 1934—three years before her death—is guarded, providing very few direct insights into her fiction. And *The Writing of Fiction* is more valuable for her critical perceptions of the works of other novelists than it is for critical introspection about her own work. In her journal, particularly the one she kept during her affair with Morton Fullerton, and in her letters to personal friends, Edith recorded her personal and literary thoughts with somewhat more frankness.

Though Edith acquired in adulthood the outward manner of self-assurance and decisiveness, she remained basically as guarded as she had been in her teens. It would seem that the effect, on her sensitive nature, of the essentially repressive way she was raised left an enduring character trait. As far as her fiction is concerned, only in her later and inferior novels did she directly reveal anything of herself, and then she revealed a querulous anger at a world that had passed her by. In her best fiction, on the other hand, she was practically always in complete intellectual and artistic command of her material, effectively excluding direct revelation of self and personality.

Even as she continued in her later years to write novels

and stories at an undiminished pace—pausing to wonder why she was sometimes tired—Edith was grieved by the increasing number of deaths among her lifelong friends. There were many such friends, not excluding her household servants, for to those whom she liked, Edith was loyal and generous to an extreme, almost to a fault. Lacking family, except for her ex-sister-in-law Minnie Jones and the latter's daughter Beatrix, Edith derived spiritual and social sustenance from her circle of friends. In fact she found much to admire in the French custom of presiding over a *salon*, and she adapted it to her own needs and circumstances in her homes both in northern and southern France.

As a result of a chill, fever, and exhaustion, Edith suffered a near-fatal illness in 1929. She took precautions and rested a bit more, but she by no means ceased her traveling and socializing, nor, as we have seen, her writing. A second illness, perhaps a mild stroke, in 1935—Edith was then seventy-three years old—still did not have the effect of significantly lessening her personal and professional activity, except for the period of the convalescence itself. But in May 1937, en route from the Riviera to her home north of Paris, while stopping at the home of her long-ago collaborator, Ogden Codman, Edith had another, more severe stroke. She was transported by ambulance to her own home, and here she lingered on for another two months, conscious and rational and apparently quite reconciled to her death. She died in August. Her coffin was attended by French war veterans, some of whom were her neighbors and all of whom recognized her generosity and devotion in serving the French cause and in ministering to bereaved and uprooted French women and children in the awful days of World War I, a war that finally doomed the society which had been so integral a part of Edith's life.

2

The Age of Innocence (1920)

With the end of World War I in 1918, Edith Wharton's world came to an end. That prewar world was characterized by, among other things, the assumption that all, or almost all, was right with the world, and that what was not right could be made so. This assumption Wharton shared to a considerable degree. She also shared the assumption, which was rapidly becoming unpopular, that difference in social class was inherently and morally justified. Specifically, she continued to believe that the mores of her own class and era were inherently—owing to social prerogative if not divine right—superior to all other mores.

By 1919, clinging to such assumptions, the fifty-seven-year-old Wharton, already an expatriate, was also losing touch with the contemporary world. *The Age of Innocence* is a palpable reaching back, a bridge to that now vanished New York City society of her adolescence. It is not, however, an indulgence in fictional nostalgia pure and simple, for it is at once loving and critical. For her material she relied not only on her own excellent memory of people and places, but on meticulous research of events, some of it conducted for her in New York by Minnie Jones. And indeed, the resemblance between her fictive names and the names of real people, friends and relatives who lived in the New York of the 1870s, is suggestively close.

We can identify the two souls in Wharton's breast (she

was familiar with Goethe's formulation of the divided self)
with the two principal characters in the novel. Newland
Archer accepts his New York society, even though he
understands it well enough to smile at it. Ellen Olenska, on
the other hand, has fled from it, has become Europeanized,
and returns to New York as an outsider, a rebel, quite
baffled at the local tribal customs. (Wharton was an eager
student of anthropology.)

Newland would have probably spent his life in a complacent, predestined way within his society, were it not for
the arrival of Ellen almost on the eve of the announcement
of his engagement to May Welland. Ellen Olenska was born
Ellen Mingott in New York. A cousin of May's, Ellen is of
proper family, although it is a family that includes more
than a few black sheep—all excommunicated from the tribe
proper, seldom mentioned, and then only in certain tones.
Ellen's parents had been roamers. After they died, she was
taken under the wing of an aunt who was a roamer too.
Ellen married a Count Olenski, a Pole, who seemed, however, to be more at home in France and Italy than in War-
saw. Very wealthy, he was also a blackguard. On discovering
the latter, Ellen fled his luxurious and corrupt menage to
return, at about age thirty, to New York City.

Ellen has a slight French accent, she is more an outsider than a New Yorker, and she is legally a married
woman living apart from her husband. Imagine her, of all
people, appearing in an opera box in a dress slightly more
daring than what New York was wearing that year! From
the beginning, Newland likes Ellen. She is like a breath of
fresh air in the oppressive ingrown society of New York.
Her very presence makes him wonder if he ought to go
through with his marriage to May Welland.

May is attractive too, but she is staid and already completely predictable. She has been trained—Wharton uses the
word repeatedly—to the role of wife and mother expected of

her by society, and it is a role she has no wish to escape or even to modify. Her treatment of Ellen derives from this training: she is kind, even solicitous in private, yet she resents Ellen's appearing in public, quite in accord with the tribal verdict—which Newland at first shares:

> . . . to receive Countess Olenska in the family circle was a different thing from producing her in public, at the opera of all places, and in the very box with the young girl whose engagement to him, Newland Archer, was to be announced within a few weeks.

Newland, however, abandons the fatuousness of his peers and begins to see Ellen in a different light when her family enlists his services as a gentleman lawyer in obtaining a divorce settlement for Ellen. His chivalric spirit rises, he sees Ellen as a victim of a cruel husband and an equally cruel alien legal system that treats a wife as practically the property of her husband with no rights of her own. There are at least three ironies in this initial acquaintance of Newland and Ellen, and we can take them to indicate that the novel is to be more than merely nostalgic. First, it is the family, the tribe, who bring the two together. Second, Newland's chivalric spirit, precursor to love, is part and parcel of his societal training. Third, Ellen's rights as a person are in fact hardly better protected in New York than in Europe.

Newland's desire to help Ellen very soon blossoms into love. Ellen, warm-hearted and open, responds. Under her almost magical influence, Newland adopts her view that the individual is more important than the tribe. But Ellen, equally open to the persuasive influence of love, reciprocally adopts a basic part of Newland's—and his society's—credo: for the sake of one's own happiness one does not inflict unhappiness on another. And she applies that specifically to herself vis-à-vis May Welland. May, less sensitive to the personal implications of this credo, twice unnecessarily outdoes Ellen, who has already renounced her love for New-

land. In justice to May, however, it must be added that she
is primarily concerned with prevailing over Newland, whose
renunciation of Ellen is still far from complete. In the first
instance, May is conspicuously willing to contravene the
tribal custom and to shorten rather spectacularly the length
of her engagement. In the second instance, after the marriage, when Newland is still prepared to desert her for Ellen,
May resorts to the time-honored expedient of announcing
her pregnancy.

The tribe, which had brought Ellen and Newland together in the first place, learns with amazing speed of the
seriousness of their affection. (Gossip is a highly developed
tribal art.) Newland is thenceforth frozen out of the tribe's
deliberations and decisions concerning Ellen. So smooth is
the freeze-out that Newland, who ought to have known the
terrain better but who in any case is not given to decisive
action, does not even realize what has happened until after
he has lost the opportunity to rescue Ellen.

Just as Ellen first appeared before the tribe at a social
ceremony—which is what the opera was turning into in the
1870s—so she is read out of the tribe, banished, at another
and equally impressive social ceremony. This is the farewell
dinner that May gives for her departing cousin—departing,
because the tribe has consigned Ellen back to Europe. Newland is obliged to witness and to be part of the cruel rite, a
metaphorical disposal feast which effectively underlines
Wharton's familiarity with the anthropology of primitive
societies, as well as with New York society. It is one of her
most moving episodes. Each member of the tribe, even while
observing the superficial amenities, plays his or her ritual
role in destroying the vulnerable member of the pair who
have outraged their customs. Suddenly, belatedly, Newland
realizes that all of them think he and Ellen are lovers, that
they have rallied around his wife in order to separate him
from his partner in guilt. Ellen is to be obliterated, socially
speaking; he is to be rehabilitated.

It was the old New York way of taking life "without effusion of blood": the way of people who dreaded scandal more than disease, who placed decency above courage, and who considered that nothing was more ill-bred than "scenes," except the behavior of those who gave rise to them.

In a final chapter that functions as an epilogue, Wharton shows us Newland a quarter of a century later, now a widower. He has played his role in his society, rather more actively than most, serving in a variety of political, municipal, and philanthropic posts. He is visiting Paris with his grown son Dallas, who has arranged for both of them to meet Ellen, now widowed and living in Paris. As Newland twenty-some years ago had more than once consciously refrained from taking the decisive, the courageous step toward Ellen, so even now he demurs. He sits on a bench under the trees and watches as his son goes to keep the appointment that had been made for both of them. Newland observes to himself that it is more real to him to stay thus than to go to see her.

Although Ellen surely stands in no need of rescuing now, Newland's reaction is very much the same as it was when she did. And Ellen, at about age thirty, was very much worth rescuing. To her, perhaps more than to any other Wharton heroine, the modern reader can relate. She is intelligent, pretty in a gypsy-like way—but not beautiful—vivacious, sensitive, and honest. She has the "mysterious faculty of suggesting tragic and moving possibilities outside the daily run of experience." Her refusal to dissemble only exacerbates her difficult relationship with the tribal mores and the people who adhere rigorously to these mores. Her mysterious faculty of suggesting unusual possibilities in life is anathema to an ingrown society devoted to preserving the traditional and the predictable, to regarding facade as reality. She asks Newland: "Does no one want to know the truth here?" No. Truth is in fact the basic taboo.

Ellen's indiscretions—wearing a becoming rather than a

modish dress, initiating conversations with men at parties, calling the tribal members at large, as well as the forms of society, dull—proceed from her honesty. But the indiscretions are slight—a flirtatious gesture, a fan brushed in passing against Newland's knees, honest eyes, even a warm kiss. Ellen resolutely avoids any situation that might lead to love-making, or—her concession to the importance of facade—even give the appearance of the possibility of love-making.

When Ellen begs Newland to inform her of the pitfalls in the New York society that seems alien and unnatural to her, it is her own honest perceptions of that society that prick the bubble of Newland's complacent acceptance and that open his eyes to its falseness. Not maliciously does Ellen tear aside the veil—that would not be her nature—but inadvertently, in the course of her almost naive observations. For her apparently sophisticated outlook is based on what seems to her the simpler European model. One may add to Ellen's admirable deeds and qualities her protecting, at risk to herself, the reputation of the secretary who aided her in her flight from Count Olenski, and her genuine thankfulness for the haven that New York at first seems to be. She could easily believe that she was "dead and buried and this dear old place is heaven." A false heaven, as she discovers, but she accepts without bitterness the suffering that "this dear old place" thrusts upon her.

The reader is likely to wish that Newland would try to sweep Ellen off her feet. But he is too much the Wharton hero to be so enterprising. It is worth noting, however, that he is not only one of the few male protagonists, but also one of the few males who is not depicted as a static character in Wharton's oeuvre. He develops under the lively immediate influence of Ellen Olenska. It is hardly an oversimplification when Louis Auchincloss declares that "Ellen Olenska turns Newland Archer from a stuffed shirt into a man." He develops emotionally as well as in terms of insight into his tribal society. Even the somewhat stuffy Newland of his pre-Ellen days is capable of accurate self-assessment: "Archer tried to console himself with the thought that he was not quite such an ass as Larry Lefferts . . . but the difference was after all one of intelligence and not of standards." And again, although by now Newland's broader perception reflects his burgeoning relationship with Ellen: ". . . the whole of New York is dying of inanition."

Newland's perception of himself, as well as of Ellen's role in opening his eyes and his heart, is epitomized in his remark: "You [Ellen] gave me my first glimpse of a real life and at the same moment you asked me to go on with a sham one." We interpret real life to imply emotional development in relation to Ellen and development as a social being through participation in the institutions of society. The sham life is a life of unemotional tranquility and traditionality (he is thinking here of May), one characterized by an aloofness from participation.

Newland's emotional perceptions develop first. So far as active commitment goes, he is heir to the belief of post-Civil War New York City society (the same one that eschewed the commercial initiative of its forebears) that politics is the arena of the political boss and the immigrant, that a gentleman remains aloof from such things. Ellen remonstrates with him about such aloofness. Years later he permits himself to be encouraged to take the plunge into politics.

But it is not till the epilogue that we discover the extent of Newland's involvements in social activity more broadly construed. Not many, not, perhaps, great, nor even consistent, but still some—although Wharton seems to downgrade this significant portion of Newland's life by compressing it into barely two pages of reminiscing by Newland. At the urging of Theodore Roosevelt (Roosevelt and Wharton knew and admired each other), he entered politics, running for the State Assembly. He was elected once. Failing of reelection, he "dropped back thankfully into obscure if useful municipal work and from that again to the writing of

occasional articles in one of the reforming weeklies that
were trying to shake the country out of its apathy."

Active in every new philanthropic, municipal, or artistic movement in New York City, Newland became sought
after by those who valued his opinion and wanted the cachet
of his name. He started a school for crippled children; he
played a major role in "reorganizing the Museum of Art,
founding the Grolier Club, inaugurating the new Library, or
getting up a new society of chamber music." Were it not for
having known Ellen Olenska, he would most likely have
done none of these things. And in doing them he does differ
markedly from the man he was at the beginning of the
novel.

 If Ellen is outside the pale of tribal society, and if
Newland, within the pale, is atypical in his perceptions and
activities, May is the tribal member par excellence. As Blake
Nevius puts it, she "personifies all the evasions and compromises of his clan; she is the 'safe' alternative." May has
been trained to go to any lengths to ignore the unpleasant.
Her innocence is the innocence in the title of the novel, the
kind that, in Wharton's words, "seals the mind against imag-
ination and the heart against experience." It is an innocence
that does not exclude, in May's case, an awareness of the
advantage of a feigned reluctance during courtship or of the
prescribed long engagement itself, any more than it excludes
a calculated shortening of that engagement, or even complic-
ity in the hypocritical banishment of Ellen. Her own welfare
is inextricably bound up with the preservation of the social
status quo. To her dying day May thoroughly believes that
the world is full of harmonious households such as her
own—and such as she perceived that of her parents to have
been. A good mother, to all outward appearances, she is
never in tune with her children. Of trends more recent than
those of her own childhood she has no comprehension.

Other representatives of the age of innocence, although
they may play lesser roles, are also quite finely drawn.

(Several appear elsewhere in Wharton's fiction.) There is, for example, Catherine Mingott, "Catherine the Great," Ellen's and May's grandmother, a liberated matriarch with a record of youthful travel in Europe; Mrs. Lemuel Struthers, widow of the shoe-polish king; Henry van der Luyden, social arbiter and descendant of Dutch patroons; Julius Beaufort, of uncertain origin and great wealth, now on the periphery of proper society; Larry Lefferts, arbiter of "form" and inveterate womanizer; and old Sillerton Jackson, who deals expertly with gossip, allowing his prejudices full sway in the *other* process. Wharton treats Catherine Mingott, and to some *characters* extent Julius Beaufort, with affectionate irony. In the case of others, for example, Sillerton Jackson, she is closer to satire:

Mr. Jackson had helped himself to a slice of the tepid filet which the mournful butler had handed him with a look as sceptical as his own, and had rejected the mushroom sauce after a scarcely perceptible sniff. He looked baffled and hungry, and Archer reflected that he would probably finish his meal on Ellen Olenska.

The last sentence above points ahead, of course, to the ritual farewell feast at which the tribe disposes of Ellen.

What is to be made of the fact that all of Newland's laudable, if modest, civic accomplishments are accorded barely two retrospective pages? It seems almost as though Wharton were uncomfortable with them. She seemed primarily to have been concerned with nostalgically recording a social change, for which Newland's activities function almost as metaphor. Social change is the point and the context of the final chapter, the epilogue, twenty-six years after Ellen returned to Europe, and twenty-six years after May blushingly hinted at her first pregnancy—thus very close to the turn of the century. Newland is sitting alone in his library.

It is here, Newland reflects, that most of the "real things" of his life had happened: May's hint of her preg-

nancy, their son's first steps, their daughter's announcement
of her engagement, discussions with May about the future of
their children, Roosevelt's persuading him to run for the
Assembly. Newland has just returned from the inauguration
of the great new galleries of the Metropolitan Museum of
Art. At the inauguration a visitor made some casual observations that revealed familiarity with what one of the galleries
looked like twenty-six years ago. These remarks trigger Newland's reminiscences about what things were like then and
his reflections about how things are now.

Young women of the present generation will smile at
May's circumlocutory announcement of her pregnancy.
That son, Dallas, becomes an architect; young men of his
generation felt free to enter politics, to become archaeolo-
gists and engineers, to follow a wide range of professions.
May, whose picture is still on Newland's desk, does not
realize that even during her lifetime "the world of her youth
had fallen into pieces and rebuilt itself." Newland does
know, but he also still believes "there was good in the old
ways." Good, therefore, in the tribal code that prevented
him from marrying Ellen, that sacrificed Ellen for the preservation of the tribe. Good in being intolerant and hypocritical. The modern reader experiences difficulty in accepting
this.

Now, Newland reflects, New York City is different.
Dallas is engaged to marry Fanny Beaufort, daughter of the
socially dubious Julius Beaufort and his mistress become
wife, "the notorious Fanny Ring." But instead of distrusting
and resenting Fanny Beaufort when *she* returns to New
York at the age of eighteen after living in Buenos Aires and
visiting in Paris, as it did Ellen Olenska, New York society
finds Fanny Beaufort pretty, amusing, and accomplished.
Newland thinks well of his future daughter-in-law and believes the marriage will be a good one.

People accept more easily, in the early 1900s, said
Wharton, because they do not bother much with their

neighbors any more. Her nostalgic heart, if not her penetrating intellect, was with the old days and the old ways: "People nowadays were too busy—busy with reform and 'movements,' with fads and fetishes and frivolities. . . ." To this extent, then, she was presenting Newland in a mildly critical light. For he was undoubtedly, if moderately, connected with reforms and movements, although it is quite impossible to imagine him having anything to do with fads and fetishes.

Reminiscing in his library, Newland also thinks about Ellen. Although her image remains in his mind as an embodiment of everything he has missed, he never sees her or communicates again with her—with "his Fanny," as his unreserved son boldly describes Ellen, to his father's face. When father and son are together in Europe shortly after Newland's evocative reminiscing, Dallas, at the suggestion of his fiancee, whom Ellen had befriended when the latter was in Paris, calls up Ellen and arranges a time at which he and his father can call on her. Newland accompanies his son to the elegant apartment building in which she lives.

But at the last minute, as we recall, he declines to go up with Dallas: "Say I'm old-fashioned. . . ." True to his generation, Newland, despite his social development and despite his adaptability, in a matter affecting him intimately, feels more comfortable with illusion, with the mores of his own generation, than with reality, with contemporaneous mores. So, undoubtedly, did Edith Wharton.

Perhaps among the mores of his generation that he instinctively abides by is that relating to the unsuitability of pity, especially pity on the part of a man for a woman, and above all for a woman who, at least partly out of affection for him, has incurred the wrath of the tribe. Newland's fund of pity seems to have been exhausted in contemplation of the harm that Count Olenski, an outsider, did to Ellen. He seems to have precious little left for the victim of the misery that he, Newland, helped visit on her. Wharton makes no explicit point of any of this; but Newland evinces no pity

and evidently feels little enough pity for Ellen (who refuses
to indulge in self-pity). Afterward, we are told, Newland
thought of her "abstractly," which conceivably has the effect, if not the purpose, of insulating him from the feeling
of pity, not to say of guilt. He seems not to have felt the self-
reproach that her banishment, and the way it was meted out,
might be presumed to evoke in a reasonably sensitive man.

At least part of this in turn relates to the double standard of sexual morality, which Wharton does not belabor,
but whose effects are clearly on view. Newland—he is more
or less expected to—sows his wild oats before getting married; other men in his society by no means stop doing so at
that point. The key is: it is permissible on the part of men if
only it does not too violently rock the boat of the *same*
society. Ellen has sown no wild oats whatever, but her love
violently rocks the boat of *the* society. Therefore she is
thrown overboard. That custom helps preserve the male
domination of the female, the only activity at which the
male characters of *The Age of Innocence* show any vigor, as
Louis Auchincloss drily notes. One must credit Wharton
with a subtle and skillful integration of the double-standard
theme with the larger theme of bittersweet criticism of a
vanished society.

To accomplish her narrative and critical purpose,
Wharton employs a modified single point of view. It is essentially that of Newland Archer. On those infrequent occa-
sions when his perceptions might not suffice for the ironic
component of her purpose—for he is, after all, still looking
at the tribal society from within and from a man's viewpoint
—Wharton as author peers unobtrusively over his shoulder.

Wharton objected to *The Pictorial Review*'s proposed
cutting of *The Age of Innocence* to satisfy space requirements, and she was angered by the cavalier attitude toward
her writing that this implied. But the book publication by
Appleton in 1920 was accompanied by advertising hailing
her as the greatest American woman novelist. She undoubt-

edly was—one wonders, indeed, why the qualification of sex was thought necessary—and the novel fully justifies that primary rank.

Wharton's plotting, as usual, is excellent, and it is freer than usual from dependence on coincidence. She knows her material thoroughly, which seems to conduce to the finely evoked bittersweetness. Her diction is imaginative and free of clichés—the novel still reads very well indeed. The structure, from the opening opera to the closing feast, pivoted on May's interventions in the relationship between Newland and Ellen, is logically and esthetically satisfying.

It is probably quite fitting that for *The Age of Innocence*, Wharton was awarded the Pulitzer Prize in 1921, although it is also unfortunate that it came only after the original recommendation that it go to Sinclair Lewis for *Main Street* was overruled. Wharton deplored the awkward affair, sympathizing completely with Lewis. It was perhaps to be expected, given both her generosity and her critical vigor, that she would in a future novel (*The Gods Arrive*, 1932) incorporate a scathing satire of the "Pulsifer Prize."

3

The House of Mirth

The House of Mirth (1905), and its tragic heroine Lily Bart, established Edith Wharton as a famous novelist and, in her own eyes, as a professional novelist—although it was in fact her ninth published book. Never had a book published by Scribner's sold at such a rate. Within three months 140,000 copies were in print—and this was after the novel had been running serially in *Scribner's Magazine* from January through November 1905. In fact, it was the unexpected necessity of having the novel ready for the magazine at an advanced deadline date that compelled Wharton to abandon her former sporadic method of writing and to establish a professional regimen for herself: a certain number of hours each day to be devoted to writing.

Wharton turned to her own society for both the background and the subject of *The House of Mirth*. That in itself does not make it a great book—the charge of triviality has some merit, and the work is dated besides. But it is a good book, and the destruction of Lily Bart by a powerful, pitiless society is capable of moving us still. This society is not, we should note, the New York society of Wharton's early childhood, the society she insists is bourgeois, but rather its hybrid, less admirable successor. In *The House of Mirth*, as in Wharton's later girlhood, the Civil War millionaires, the industrial exploiters, the frontier freebooters, are buying and marrying their way into the tired, defenseless social estab-

lishment, whose facade of devotion to older values becomes
ever thinner.

When we first meet Lily Bart she is twenty-nine, born
to wealth and to a heritage in New York society. Lily's
original misfortune is in having profligate parents who become bankrupt, both financially and socially. Lily is well-
educated, sensitive, and frivolous, very much her parents'
daughter. The financial ruin of her father when she is nine-
teen leaves her with but one way of making a living. She will
for the time being have to become a useful companion to
women of wealth. Then she will be obliged to make a suitable marriage for money. These necessities become still
more pressing at the death of Lily's widowed aunt, who,
after the death of Lily's mother, has provided the orphaned
young woman a proper and cheerless shelter. The ultra-
respectable Mrs. Peniston, full of copy-book axioms ap-
plicable to social conduct of a half-century ago, and quite
without sympathy for Lily and her way of life, leaves her a
mere ten thousand dollars. The will is an expression of her
aunt's disapproval not only of Lily's social habits—endless
parties, dancing, gambling at bridge—and her manifest inability to manage money, but even more of Lily's breaking
her society's code of conduct for unmarried women—in this
case giving the appearance of becoming involved with a
married man.

The man is Gus Trenor. The Trenors, on the top rung
of Wharton's disintegrating (or reintegrating, depending on
the point of view) turn-of-century New York society, still
make a pretense of supporting and adhering to traditional
values. To be sure, they are ready enough to violate those
values, but not too spectacularly. Lily, beset by gambling
debts, is prevailed upon by Gus Trenor to let him make
investments in the stock market for her. He does so with, of
course, his own money. This compromises Lily hopelessly.
First, she is exposed to the unwanted amorous advances of
Trenor, who, however, can still be fended off by her appeal

to his not yet completely atrophied sense of *noblesse oblige.*
Second, she incurs the jealous enmity, not of Judy Trenor,
but of Mrs. Bertha Dorsett. (The code permits a married
woman, protected by a husband's name and money, to
dally.) Bertha, one rung lower than the Trenors, responds
by giving Lily her first push down the social ladder—the
beginning of what is to become a precipitate fall.

After eleven years of diligently acquiring social skills,
Lily thus finds herself being displaced from her ambiguous
role of being attached to, but not quite belonging to, the
highest level of society, at whose parties she is a regular,
esteemed, and occasionally exploited guest. After having
passed up one or two good marital possibilities when she
first came out in society, she more recently has passed up the
opportunity to make a most suitable marriage with a millionaire stick-in-the-mud, Percy Gryce. Subsequently, she
refuses ever-less-suitable suitors.

Perhaps Lawrence Selden is not accurately categorized
as a "suitor," but it is he with whom Lily is most com-
patible. For a stroll through a park with Selden, she breaks
an appointment with Gryce. She thus breaks with Gryce in
the broader sense too, for the sake of a brief pleasure. For
Selden cannot marry her; he knows it and she knows it. He
is not wealthy at all, by the standards of their society. Lily's
next suitor is Simon Rosedale. Intent on making a match
that will translate his immense—uninherited—wealth into a
secure position in society, Rosedale is not at all reticent in
urging upon Lily the desirability of marrying him, from her
point of view as well as from his. She declines. By the time
her less auspicious circumstances suggest that she might gain
by reconsidering her refusal, Rosedale is disinclined to renew
his offer, for Lily would no longer be useful to him: within a
year "she had lost the power to abbreviate the remaining
steps of [his] way" to a social eminence that would match
his economic eminence. Lily, knowing that his social cupid-
ity is not unmixed with a certain genuine affection for her,

wonders what would happen if she made him marry her for love alone. But, typically, her basic honesty undermines a possible route out of a social position which grows more and more untenable. If she despised Rosedale a year ago, she still dislikes him now. In the meantime, while she is an impecunious guest on a Riviera yacht cruise, as well as back in the increasingly suffocating confines of New York society, her path now and again crosses that of Selden.

As the antecedence of Lily's suitors and potential suitors has crossed the still perceptible line separating hereditary society—Selden—from the climbers—Rosedale, she is herself forced downward from one social level after another, and the downward range of her associations extends well beyond that of her romances. She descends from the hereditary nonmercantile society to that of the new investors, to the still newer moneymaking climbers, to the less affluent fringe. Toward the end she is taken under the sponsorship and the roof of Selden's cousin, Gerty Farish, a social worker, who by necessity and preference leads a dingy—Lily's word—lower middle-class life. To Gerty, Lily pours out her heart, but, despite the urgency, Lily is not capable of revealing her need for money—above all, to repay Trenor.

In Gerty's apartment, at Gerty's social level, Lily Bart is like a butterfly in a dusty jar. But her descent is not yet completed. When she was a social butterfly, one of Lily's handy talents lay in personally decorating her own hats. Now it is arranged that she shall try to make professional use of that amateur talent. The last rung of her descent is a job in a millinery workroom, a job from which she is fired for incompetence. Thence to a fatal self-administered overdose of sleeping drops, even as Lawrence Selden is coming closer to making up his mind to propose marriage. Some critics regard Lily's death as accidental. The text is not explicit, but an accidental death would not seem to be the tragic conclusion toward which Wharton has directed her story. In any case, if it is accidental, it is an intentional accident. Lily simply does not care about living any longer.

In a larger sense than Bertha Dorsett's first vicious push, what precipitates Lily's fall? It has often been described in terms of naturalistic determinism; she is the foreordained victim of her environment. This seems to account for only part of her plight, however. After eleven years of making her way in this society, "eleven years of late hours and indefatigable dancing," what is there in Lily that causes her to offend society in such a way that it spurns her? Surely her rejection of such an appropriate suitor as Percy Gryce, like her risky involvement with such a married man as Gus Trenor, is only the tip of the iceberg. She offends society not by any one or two things, really, but rather by a number of things, blunders small and large. And these blunders, these offenses, are the outward signs of a deeper personal development in Lily that accompanies and balances—one might almost say cancels—her attainment of social competence.

Partly as a result of her "long bondage to other people's pleasures," Lily becomes increasingly considerate of those who are dependent on her. She comes to feel scruples to which she was previously immune. She makes her way occasionally—not consistently—to a base of personal honesty. She heeds from time to time the voice of her authentic self in preference to the commands of social discipline. As she tries to keep faith with herself by turning down her suitors, she exposes herself to a process of entrapment and then destruction in the social jungle in which she was formerly at home and whose perilous byways she still knows, but now pays no attention to.

Lily, however, is quite unable to summon the force of will that will mobilize her awakening identity. Her authentic sense is horrified at her social self. She crystallizes her abhorrent self-image in a reference to the Furies of Aeschylus's *Eumenides*, characterizing it as "a disfigurement—some hideous change that has come to you while you slept." But within a few months the contending forces within her have

achieved a kind of balance. This is even reflected in a change
in Lily's physical appearance. In the light of Wharton's earlier observation that Lily's pliability enabled her to survive,
since pliable substances resist breaking better than do stiff
materials, her descriptive terms now are an unmistakable
omen:

Then [Lily's beauty] had had a transparency through which the
fluctuations of the spirit were sometimes tragically visible; now
the impenetrable surface suggested a process of crystallization
which had fused her whole being into one hard brilliant
substance.

Each of Lily's confrontations with her emerging consciousness, each of her bouts of honesty, leaves her a little
more brittle, a little more vulnerable to destruction by a
society which regards departures from the tribal rules, and
honesty, as weaknesses and exploits them to her disadvan-
tage. Irving Howe asserts that "Lily is pitifully lacking in
any core of personal being." Rather, it would seem that her
increasing revelation of just such a core makes her pitifully
vulnerable. But society is her habitat, and to it she gravitates
back willy-nilly, at lower and lower levels. Her fragile self-
awareness and her unassertive honesty cannot handle the
new social risks to which these very qualities keep impelling
her. Drifting, she forfeits her last chance of marriage as an
escape from her manner of life, which is conditioned by
society, or more precisely, by the code that that society
stipulates, uniquely, for the unmarried woman, as distinct
from the woman who can count on the protection of her
husband's name and money. The only escape left for Lily is
the overdose of sleeping drops.

Diana Trilling suggests an unconscious portrait of
Henry James in the fictional Lawrence Selden in *The House
of Mirth*. This is possible, although unlikely. Wharton had
barely met James in person, in May 1904. She was already
working on the novel in 1903 and she put in her most

concentrated work on it in the summer of 1904. To the extent that Lawrence Selden reflects a person outside of literature, that person is more likely to be the marriage-shy Walter Berry. It is Selden's bachelor quarters that Lily visits impulsively, but not in ignorance of society's code, twice toward the outset of the novel. The first time it is in the company of Selden, with whom she is already on friendly and sympathetic terms. Their purpose is to have tea and pleasant conversation for an hour or so while she is between trains, on her way to a house party in the country. It is a quite innocent visit, in broad daylight, but nonetheless Lily is breaking a taboo of the society to which she and Selden belong. And unfortunately she is seen as she leaves the building by Simon Rosedale, who is not yet of that society and who is not averse to pressing the advantage his knowledge gives him when he later proposes marriage to Lily.

On the occasion of her second visit, likewise during the daytime, Selden is not even at home. Still she is breaking the taboo, just the same as if he were at home. A cleaning-woman takes advantage of this and later presses a blackmail demand. Selden, genuinely attracted to Lily, could save her from the amorous and financial machinations against her by marrying her. But, a passive male of the older, hereditary layer of New York society, he seems to take refuge in avoidance, in irony, in assuming the role of raisonneur. It is impossible for him to marry Lily, we are told frequently, because he does not preside over sufficient wealth.

Here the modern reader is forced to make some adjustments in concept. For he or she will have perceived that the similarity of background, the mutual generosity of sentiment, the rapport, the sheer enjoyment of each other's company all combine to suggest that a marriage between Lawrence Selden and Lily Bart would most likely be a sound and happy one. So why should Selden's presumed lack of wealth prevent it? It must be remembered, in at least partial explanation of Selden's reluctance, that Lily's prime need—

or more exactly, what society tells her is her prime need—is not love and marriage so much as marriage and money. We can credit Selden with sensitivity to that unhappy reality. The modern reader will counter that Selden really does not seem excessively impecunious anyway. To be sure, his coat is a bit shabby, his rug a bit faded. But he turns up on the Riviera and remains for some while, apparently under no great necessity to economize. Nor in fact, despite the modest bohemianism of his lodgings, does he stint himself in New York, and we are apt to regard his rug as only very genteelly faded. In the end, we simply have to take Wharton's word for it that by the standards of the society she describes and is familiar with, Selden is not wealthy.

If, then, his reluctance to propose marriage to Lily is partly owing to his realistic (by his standards) appraisal of their situation, it must be admitted, it is also due to Selden's essentially passive character. This character type, perhaps reflecting Wharton's memory of her father or even her perception of the generality of upper-class New York males, reappears frequently in her novels. And for all his sophisticated languor, Selden is not without strong passions, as we see from his response to Lily's thinly draped appearance in a *tableau vivant.* But he declines to risk his passions, his emotions. In this he is protecting himself first of all, not Lily. Protecting himself, that is, in and from the same society that is destroying the more vulnerable Lily. When at last he discovers that she was repaying Gus Trenor the full amount of the improper loan Trenor had made her, when, in other words, Lily is eligible for vindication before the bar of society, then Selden is ready to marry her. But it is too late. She is dead.

Lily's less inhibited suitor, Simon Rosedale, plays a more consciously calculating game *vis-à-vis* Lily and society. He is an ardent suitor when she could be valuable to him, a cool acquaintance when her social value is gone. At first, indeed, Rosedale seems very much the caricature of the

aggressive Jewish businessman on the make both commer-
cially and culturally. To establish the caricature Wharton
makes obvious use of anti-Semitic clichés. It would probably
be inaccurate to infer, as some have done, anti-Semitism
extending beyond that inherent in the use of such clichés.
(Her record in the case of blacks has little to justify it except
the plea that that was a different era.) Rosedale, in any case,
emerges somewhat from the burden of cliché as the novel
develops. He does not, one must admit, develop into a particularly admirable man in his later relationship with Lily.
But he does have shadings of complexity. It is true that he is
given to a leering, ruthless willingness to take advantage of
his knowledge of, and relationship to, Lily. When he suggests, ungrammatically (Wharton's most concise signal of
nonsociety origins), that he and Lily could be good friends,
Lily retorts: "What is your idea of being good friends? . . .
Making love to me without asking me to marry you?" Rosedale answers: "Well, that's about the size of it, I suppose."
On the other hand, when he meets up with Lily when she is
ill and near the end of her miserable job in the millinery
workroom, Rosedale rises to a considerateness that is almost
poignant in proffering tea and sympathy.

Wharton portrays sharply the members of the several
social layers through which Lily sinks to the intolerable level
of the workroom. Bertha Dorsett's antecedence is as pedi-
greed as that of the Trenors, but Bertha no longer makes
even the pretense of caring about the traditional values. In
revenge for Lily's closeness to Gus Trenor, Bertha abandons
Lily heartlessly to Carrie Fisher, whose specialty is being a
guide to the new rich eager to pay for admission to society.
Perhaps simply because her devotion to materialistic values
is so frank, perhaps because she is helpful to Lily, Carrie
emerges as rather more likable than Bertha. Her help to Lily
consists in arranging the latter's transfer to a refuge with the
Wellington Brys, who are very rich and very, very eager for
admission to the upper reaches. And so on, down through

two or three more levels until Lily arrives in the workroom, which we—and quite likely the illustrator of the 1905 edition—appropriately envision as being in a basement, and which Wharton describes as an "underground of toilers."

This underground, however, Wharton describes in terms much less angry and bitter than those which she reserves for the members of the social hierarchy. It will strike the reader, too, that she spares Gerty Farish, Selden's social-worker cousin and Lily's confidante, from her rather pervasive authorial bitterness. To be sure, Gerty's environment and life Wharton characterizes as dingy, in evident contrast to the bright and wealthy environment and life that Lily quests after. Lawrence Selden, as we have gathered, by no means escapes Wharton's acerbity. Nor, most to the point, does Lily herself, even as she is simultaneously accorded a deep and genuine compassion.

If *The House of Mirth* enjoyed a huge popular success, its critical reception was by no means unanimously enthusiastic. Its major weakness from our present point of view is precisely what contemporaneous critics faulted it for: it dealt too much with the petty affairs of a trivial society—however tragic the fate of the victim of such a society. This society still existed in 1905 and was apparently interesting to readers, if less so to critics. A parallel might be found in the present fascination with the lives of "the beautiful people," which is rather like the fascination expressed by Lily's millinery coworkers. Lily and her kind were discussed with a "mixture of insatiable curiosity and contemptuous freedom." The social values in *The House of Mirth* are alien today; the novel runs the risk of being quaint. What saves it, what makes it enjoyable to modern readers, is Wharton's allusive and ironic style, aided by a rich vocabulary, and her bitter scorn of a materialistic and indifferent society.

That society, Wharton's society, victimizes women far more grievously than it does men. Wharton knew this and her novel declared this. Lily Bart is at least partly a reflection of Wharton. The original title of the dramatic sketch that later was to become *The House of Mirth* was "A Moment's Ornament," which tellingly denotes the role assigned to women in this society—not merely ornamental, but briefly ornamental. If the title has been changed, the theme remains in *The House of Mirth*: "She [Lily] had been fashioned to adorn and delight; to what other end does nature round the rose-leaf and paint the humming-bird's breast?"

And years later Wharton apparently finds the plight of women as bad or worse. She believes "women were made for pleasure and procreation." By itself the last statement may be taken two ways: as a credo, or as a reluctant and bitter description of the status quo. In consideration of *The House of Mirth*, the latter interpretation seems the more likely. Lily Bart's whole training has been to be an agreeable and transient ornament. Over-trained, over-specialized, Lily lacks the ability either to adapt and, in adapting, survive, or to escape —except of course the escape of death. Unlike men, she cannot flee to the west, she cannot even get a decent job. As an unmarried woman she is an almost completely helpless ornament. Married, she would be less helpless but hardly less ornamental.

NB.

4

The Custom of the Country

The Custom of the Country was published in book form in 1913; Wharton had been working on it intermittently since spring of 1908. It began appearing serially in *Scribner's Magazine* in January 1913, but even at that date she still had not completed it. R. W. B. Lewis designates it as "her most substantial and far-reaching novel, and one that introduced the most restless and devastating of her heroines." The exuberance of that judgment of the novel may call forth objections—certainly it is a masterly novel—but that view of the heroine is quite unexceptionable.

The heroine is Undine Spragg, an ironic enough name, although when Wharton was pressed to explain her use of this and similar "unlikely" names in *The Custom of the Country*, she responded by citing real names every bit as unlikely. In any case the disharmony between Undine's richly allusive first name and her spare, monosyllabic last name seems to hint strongly at irony. The novel records the progress of this redoubtable heroine step by step, affair by affair, marriage by marriage, from middle-class society in Apex City (more nomenclatural irony) to the peak, or very close to the peak, of international high society in Europe.

The Custom of the Country is a long novel, almost six hundred pages in the 1913 edition. Wharton divides it into five books. In the first book, or more precisely, two years before it begins, the Spraggs, father, mother, and daughter,

leave Apex, the source of Mr. Spragg's ill-gotten but perfectly legal wealth, because Undine has outgrown the place
and because of the scandal attending the dissolution of her
two-week-long marriage to Elmer Moffatt. Abner Spragg is
always trying to bribe his indifferent daughter into loving
him more. The relocation of the family from comfortable
and familiar Apex City to unknown and inhospitable New
York City is at bottom one more such bribe. Critics vari-
ously locate Apex City in Kansas and in Nebraska. The
distinction probably is not important; it is all *terra incognita*
to Wharton, who relied on newspaper clippings for her information about the midwest. The result, filtered through
her New York point of view, is a grotesque never-never
land—which, however, serves her contrastive purpose well
as the geographical and cultural background of the Spraggs,
late of Apex, now of New York. (Wharton's New York
point of view is pervasive: she even has a train steaming *out
of*, rather than away from, the Reno station.)

After a period of failure and frustration on the fringes
of New York society, the Spraggs follow other midwestern
émigrés in taking up residence in the vulgar splendor of the
Hotel Stentorian—a mistaken avenue to social acceptance,
as Undine later realizes. Undine shows more capacity than
her parents for learning the social ropes; she gradually ac-
quires enough knowledge to gain some acceptance. But it is
only when she also contrives to gain a husband from that
society that her acceptance is complete. She marries Ralph
Marvell. Each partner clearly recognizes what the other
brings to this marriage. But their incompatibility is, of
course, monumental.

The second book begins some four months after the
marriage. Undine and Ralph are on a European honeymoon
and already their dissimilar backgrounds and temperaments
are leading to misunderstandings and conflicts—in which
Ralph, still clinging to a romantic vision of his bride, always
yields. He would prefer to tarry in an isolated villa in the

hills near Siena, while Undine wants to go to Saint Moritz, where the crowds gather. "We'll go wherever you please," Ralph agrees, "you make every place the one place." The honeymoon is cut short—after several months—because Abner Spragg's market speculations have soured to the point that he cannot send the honeymooners any more money. And the contributions from Ralph's family cannot be increased, for their wealth by no means matches their social position. Undine is learning the value of money in a more specific way, but that scarcely heals the rift in her marriage. Back in New York she contrives to have an affair with a member of one of the first families, wealthier than Ralph's family, the crude and egotistical Peter Van Degen.

In the third book, Undine, in Paris now and abandoned by Van Degen, divorces Ralph, leaving a two-year-old son in his temporary custody. (She had resented the child ever since her pregnancy.) Ralph, upon receiving final word from Undine that she intends to divorce him, is overcome by a dream-like trance or fantasy suffused by an array of water-metaphors based on the identification of Undine with the water nymph who bore her name originally. This episode is one of Wharton's rare evocations of allusive fantasy other than in her short stories. As Ralph is thwarted and repelled in his efforts to catch the waves (Undine's name is also related to the French word for "wave"), he is cruelly pushed down in the water. But still he "floated, danced on the fiery waves of pain. . . ." Ultimately his fantasy returns him to dry land. "He woke on a stony beach. . . . He felt the ecstasy of decreasing pain. . . . The beach was his own bed."

Undine tries to reconcile herself to being abandoned by Van Degen with the rationalization that she had learned "a lesson almost worth the abasement": it is a mistake for a woman to take money from a man to whom she is not married. She pursues, attracts, and marries Raymond de Chelles, scion of an aristocratic French family that could trace its history back for centuries. As Undine's marriage to

Ralph Marvell had propelled her to the top of New York society, so now her marriage to the Marquis de Chelles elevates her instantly to the summit of Parisian society. Chelles is not capable of understanding the unpleasant truth about Undine's motives; for that, a Peter Van Degen or an Elmer Moffatt is required.

The fourth book for the most part takes leave of Undine and dwells on the life of Ralph Marvell after the divorce. The face of life has changed for him. He adapts as best he can. Disillusioned, languishing in a kind of acedia, he takes up the suggestions of relatives and friends that he ought to write. "He no longer saw life on the heroic scale: he wanted to do something in which men should look no bigger than the insects they were." Writing a novel was one of only two concerns he now had; the other was raising his son Paul. For the first he lacks the vision, the talent, and the self-discipline; for the second, he has the sensitivity and the love. His possessive attitude toward the boy is easily forgivable in the face of Undine's machinations, now that Paul is at a less troublesome age, to obtain custody to "give her the appearance of respectability."

In order to obtain funds beyond what the limited family reserve can provide him, Ralph falls in with Elmer Moffatt, now on the rise as a financier in New York. In the course of their association, Elmer lets fall word of his youthful secret marriage with Undine and of the divorce that shortly followed. From the blows he has suffered, of which Elmer's crude revelation is the climax, Ralph's never vigorous powers of resistance collapse. He can stand no more. "He said to himself: 'My wife . . . this will make it all right for her . . .' and a last flash of irony twitched through him." He puts a revolver to his head, to a carefully selected spot behind his ear. To the degree that Elmer Moffatt is the catalyst of Ralph's suicidal intent, the suicide, as E. K. Brown observes, is a symbol of the defeat of the old aristocracy by the new plutocracy.

The fifth book begins with Undine, now the Marquise de Chelles, at the height of her social and material power, and therefore of her happiness. It is not long, however, before the constraining realities and duties of French family life are borne in on her. As that occurs, she is progressively estranged from the Chelles family. For here, Undine learns, the individual counts for nothing except as a member of the family, the clan, to which she must submit and for whose benefit she must sacrifice her individuality. As long as she is part of the family, her resistance to these family demands, however much they resemble in kind, if not degree, those of Ralph's family, is futile. For her new husband has the advantage of a stronger personality as well as of a stronger tradition.

The confrontations between Undine and Raymond come to a climax when he discovers her involvement in trying to arrange the sale of some tapestries that had been given to the Chelles by Louis XV—just so much old clutter to Undine. The prospective purchaser turns out to be Elmer Moffatt. (This negotiation prefigures Undine's own later return to Moffatt as his wife.) The inevitable divorce takes place. Such a step, however, is a terrible affront to the mores of her adopted society, an error she quickly recognizes. She is demoted to the level of balneatory society, consisting largely of wealthy unattached Americans and Europeans belonging to the aristocracy of the second and third ranks, who frequent the spas and health resorts of the continent. Still, as we by now know she will, Undine recovers the lost ground and gains some besides. She remarries Elmer Moffatt, whose financial chicanery has carried him to the heights of international society. He is being considered for appointment as an ambassador. Undine has access to virtually anything money can buy. That, she discovers to her sorrow, excludes three things she would dearly like to have. She has forfeited her claim to the respect of the hereditary social aristocracy in New York and Paris; she has no chance for

the love of her son, now nine years old, who loves his
adopted father Raymond de Chelles; finally, her status as a
divorced woman makes her present husband ineligible for
the ambassadorship to which his money otherwise entitles
him.

Blake Nevius describes Undine Spragg as "the perfect
flowering of the new materialism. . . . the most egocentric
and dehumanized female in American fiction." An assessment in at least approximately those terms proceeds inevitably from the sum of the events described above. She is
also cold, ruthless, and completely selfish. As a child, she
may have come close to feeling something akin to love for
her father, if we are right in detecting a residual affection in
her banter with him. She hates her mother. In these relationships we seem to find reflected and grossly exaggerated the
relationships Wharton had as a child with her own parents.
Wharton, indeed, seems to be not without a small measure
of sympathy for Undine during the latter's initial residence
in New York—for her following false trails to success, for
her mortifications. But whatever slight authorial sympathy
there might have been is gradually withdrawn, so that Undine becomes more and more a kind of dehumanized abstraction in her unswerving desire for possessions and
comfort.

Undine unblushingly gears her personal relationships to
that end. Her friendships, her love affairs, her marriages are
invariably superficial. Not once is she concerned with love,
of which she is in any case practically incapable. Marriages are simply the means by which she can advance up
the social ladder to wealth and comfort. It must be noted,
however—which male critics rarely do—that marriages are
in fact the only means at her disposal, as a woman, to get
where she wants to go. The male arrivistes—Elmer Moffatt
and Abner Spragg come to mind—have far more latitude:
work, market speculation, politics, influence peddling. From
these realms society excludes the woman. This observation is

not meant as an apology for Undine. In terms of traditional morality, her aims are scarcely exalted ones. But in the context of a society that does exalt materialism above all else, it should not be too surprising that, given her ambitiousness, she adopts a materialistic code of values. No one would tax Undine with being intellectual, or even much more than functionally literate—she had read no new book but *When the Kissing Had to Stop*, "of which [her hostess] seemed not to have heard." But we cannot deny her perceptiveness and flexibility in determining and exploiting, often by trial-and-error, the one avenue by which she can achieve her aims.

For all her emotional sterility and for all her being "what the gods had made her"—that is, an ambitious woman in a materialistic and chauvinistic society—Undine is not simply a static character who confronts and prevails over a number of obstacles en route to success. She develops social adeptness, she learns continually. She learns to advance in society by constant and usually skillful application of one-upmanship.

In this sense, as Nevius suggests, *The Custom of the Country* is rather like a novel of roguery and Undine is rather like a *pícara*. Certainly the larger purpose of the picaresque novel, that is, social satire, is amply fulfilled in *The Custom of the Country*. And like a *pícara*, Undine learns the foibles of the society that is her hunting ground, and she gulls its members with all the élan of Francisco López de Ubeda's prototypical *pícara* Justina Díaz. The honest, the dull, and the innocent are usually no match for her. To be sure, true to the tradition of the *pícara*, she is not completely immune from error—but she does not make the same error twice. Her origins do not lie in the lower levels of society, as one expects from a genuine picaresque heroine. On the other hand, from the points of view of the societies on both sides of the Atlantic that she crashes and exploits, Apex City is distinctly inferior—but only materially, not

morally. In fact, the lines of social demarcation are far more
in flux in *The Custom of the Country* than they would be in
a true picaresque novel. We find, as a result or at least as a
concomitant of this flux, a relaxed morality prevalent at a
variety of social levels. Undine lives easily in the midst of
this fluid morality. Perhaps the greatest difference between
Undine and a traditional *pícara* lies in her absolute lack of a
sense of humor. She is amoral, reckless, and predatory—and
humorless.

Undine also falls short of being a fully developed character. Critics have seized on her one-sided array of character
traits and denounced her as a monster, an abstraction. Let
us however bear in mind that despite her being one-sided,
possibly a monster or an abstraction, she does develop over
the length of the novel, by persistence, by observation, and
by experience, from an at least slightly pitiable outsider to a
very solidly entrenched insider.

Undine as an insider knows what is going on, as it
affects her, although Wharton rises to heights of satire in
telling us so:

When Raymond de Chelles ceased to be interested in her conversation she had concluded that it was the way of husbands;
but since then it had been slowly dawning on her that she
produced the same effect on others. Her entrances were always
triumphs; but they had no sequel. As soon as people began to
talk they ceased to see her. Any sense of insufficiency exasperated
her, and she had vague thoughts of cultivating herself, and
went so far as to spend a morning in the Louvre and go to one
or two lectures by a fashionable philosopher. But though she
returned from these expeditions charged with opinions, their
expression did not excite the interest she had hoped. Her views,
if abundant, were confused, and the more she said the more
nebulous they seemed to grow.

Typically, Wharton's satire is couched in understatement or
plain statement of damning details; the statement usually

includes a scattering of linguistic ironies as well, as "fashionable" (one of her favorites), "expeditions," "charged," and "abundant" in the above passage.

Finally, we may wish to speculate about what makes Undine run on her own particular course, leaving discarded husbands in her wake. She wants wealth and comfort, yes, but what makes her want these things so avidly? Her goal is always to have more—and ever more—material possessions and comfort. Her character, as we have noted, is one-sided, defective. Certainly we are justified in assuming it was hopelessly stunted by her early environment in such a way that she is blind to all goals but the one she saw about her at every hand, to the exclusion of all others: materialism. Since she is a woman, the avenues by which *she* can pursue this goal in accord with her considerable ambition are very much restricted by society. She takes the one avenue open to her, and becomes an expert on the terrain it covers. Of course, the goal of material fulfillment always seems just a little bit further on. She would perhaps finally be closing in on it as an ambassador's wife. But her experiences along the way, her divorces, each seemingly necessary in its time, have the final ironic effect of barring her from being an ambassador's wife, "the one part she was really made for."

If the one-sidedness of Undine's character makes her an easy target of satire, brings her close to being a caricature, what are we to say of her parents? So exaggerated are their characterizations that we are hard put to accept either Abner or Leota Spragg seriously. The former is a crude hustler who became a pillar of society in Apex City, once he accumulated some wealth. That was not difficult in Apex City for a man of his ambition, talents, and morality. A typhoid epidemic had claimed the lives of both of Undine's siblings. This tragedy, "by causing Mr. Spragg to resolve that thereafter Apex should drink pure water, had led directly to the founding of his fortunes." For he played a leading role in the Pure

Water Movement, which bought at an advantageous price
some land he had taken on a bad debt, and which caused to
be built on this land a reservoir and a water-works. Mr.
Spragg grew rich and powerful. New York City, however,
proves to be beyond his depth both financially and socially.
And later, in Europe, Undine is happy enough to dissociate
herself from the touristic maladroitness of her parents and
send them back to the United States.

In the social sphere, Mrs. Spragg is of a kind with her
husband. As to his financial ventures, she professes ignorance and lack of interest. But she can divine from the
expression on his face when stock-market reverses are apt to
curtail her self-indulgent life style. Although Mrs. Spragg is
always the first to succumb to her daughter's arguments—in
the early days inevitably involving the expenditure of family
funds—she is not rewarded for that with the slightest trace
of daughterly affection. Undine, in any case, outgrows her
parents—first her mother, then her father—much as she
outgrew Apex City. If we have any feelings for them at all,
it is most likely one of pity for their lot as early discards
along Undine's road to material and social preeminence.

Ralph Marvell, Undine's second husband, is accorded
similar treatment: when his usefulness to her declines, he is
discarded. Ralph, however, is presented in a far more complex and sympathetic way. In fact, the structure of the novel
allows us to suppose that Wharton's heart is very much with
him. For almost the entire fourth book is an excursus devoted to Ralph's life—and death—after Undine leaves him,
and has little to do with Undine, who is, after all, the heroine of the novel. Ralph represents Wharton's own gentle,
aristocratic, fatuous New York society that preceded the
incursions of the Invaders from places like Apex City.

In that invaded New York, Ralph and his family are
little more than relics. He is almost like an uncomprehend-
ing visitor from another planet. A true Wharton hero, "his

profession was the least real thing in his life." Typically, his profession, or more accurately, nonprofession, is law. And while the law may well be the least real thing in his life, his is a life so full of unreality that one more unreal dimension is hardly that important. Ralph not only quotes poetry, he quotes esoteric and abstruse poetry. To make more money, for Undine and the approbation of Undine, he joins a real-estate firm. His partners tolerate him because of his advantageous social connections.

Ralph's confusion of the name "Undine" with the woman, Undine, is instructive. Undine, in legend, is a beautiful water nymph who obtains a human soul by marriage to a human being, who in turn falls madly in love with her. But love cools; pure-hearted Undine, unable to adapt to the hardness and the deviousness of human beings, returns in grief to her watery home. Ralph's pitiable insistence on forcing his bride Undine into a romantic vision he conjures up from her name and the legend attached to it, is reflected in his ever more specific allusions—during their honeymoon—to the presumed source of her name (which was actually a hair styling product invented by her grandfather). Undine's stolid inability to grasp any of his flattering allusions is a symbol of the larger tragedy of Ralph's complete inability to understand her or to adapt to her and her world.

His confusion at her lack of responsiveness to his allusions also defines his insufficiency as a creative artist. Ralph has literary ambitions; he wants to write a novel and he fancies that contemplation of a waterfall will inspire him to the necessary adjectives. Adjectives, we note, not verbs! (And this on his honeymoon!) Years later, after Undine has sued for divorce, he still dreams of writing. He sees life on a less heroic scale than formerly, "and wrote an opening chapter that struck him as not too bad." It even gives him a bit of a feeling of authority and importance. But he is unable to write much more. As an artist, as a businessman, and as a

man attempting to live in a world not of his making, Ralph
is a failure. He arouses our sympathy as does no other
character in *The Custom of the Country*.

Undine treats Raymond de Chelles, her fourth husband, with equal callousness, but he has reserves of personal
resiliency as well as a role in a family that is still strongly
bulwarked by tradition. Elmer Moffatt, Undine's first and
fifth husband, seems enigmatic, perhaps owing to an absence
of characterization. Whether as small-town lover or international financier, his eye is on the main chance. He is
unencumbered by any morality that might stand between
him and the acquisition of material wealth and pleasure. His
folk wit and his accumulation of experience along with
wealth enable him to dispense helpful homilies to those with
less luck, or more morality, but we would be mistaken in
regarding him merely as a well-heeled cracker-barrel philosopher abroad in high society. He is, in fact, a foil worthy of
Undine's mettle; it can be said with more than the usual
appropriateness that they deserve each other.

The Custom of the Country has been criticized for
structural imbalance, caused by the fourth book, devoted
chiefly to Ralph Marvell after he has been discarded by
Undine. Wharton, pressed by deadlines and beset by many
interruptions in the writing of the novel, may well have
lacked the opportunity to make cuts. (Under pressure, she
habitually wrote more pages than were needed.) It is more
likely that she wrote book four so expansively because its
material, whether or not germane to Undine's story, lay
close to Wharton's own sentiments and recollections.

From a strictly formal point of view, however, it is not
necessary to apologize for, or even explain, book four on the
basis of assumptions lying outside the novel. Were it not for
the presence of this interlude, with its evocations of tradition
and sentiment and its appeal to the reader for sympathy on
behalf of Ralph Marvell, it is just possible that *The Custom
of the Country*, for all its polished narrative technique and

astringent satire, might sink under the weight of cold, one-sided characterizations never very far from outright carica-ture. In other words, in addition to its legitimate, if rather drawn-out, suspensive function, book four functions also as a necessary counterweight to the prevailing tone of the novel as a whole. It enables us to be responsive to satire without being dulled by too much of it.

5

The Reef

The only one of Wharton's major novels that shows any
considerable influence of Henry James is *The Reef*, published in 1912. (Its publication by Appleton marked the
beginning of the end of Wharton's long association with
Scribner's.) In the case of *The Reef*, at least, she may well
be exempted from James's previous complaint that she
habitually surveyed the psychological terrain from too great
a height. For here she isolates and examines the novelistic
situation and the characters in intense and sensitive detail
and with great subtlety.

The Reef, although of only moderate length, is divided
into five books. There are from seven to ten chapters in each
book, so that the novel has a formal balance. Wharton deftly
leads the four main characters through a concentrated series
of reactions to, and interactions upon, one another in—or
mostly in—the secluded French château called Givré, and
mostly within the span of a few days. These characters are:
Anna Leath, an American widow in her late thirties, the
owner, through her late husband, of Givré; George Darrow,
an American diplomat and Anna's suitor; Owen Leath,
Anna's stepson; and Sophy Viner, an American girl from the
other side of the tracks, George's sometime girlfriend, now
governess of Anna's daughter, and soon to become Owen's
fiancee.

Although we are told that George Darrow is a diplomat, and he demonstrates diplomatic skills in the course of events at Givré, he seems, in the manner of Wharton's protagonists, to have scant commitment to professionalism. He is on leave more than on duty, as far as we can make out. On the way to Givré to renew his friendship with Anna, whom he had known before her marriage, and to ask her to marry him, he quite by chance (Wharton only rarely gets away from her disconcerting reliance on coincidence) meets a former distant acquaintance. Sophy Viner is waiting in the rain for the ferry at Dover. Since George had just received, as his train was moving from the London station, a rather curt, nonexplanatory telegram from Anna asking him to postpone his visit to Givré for two weeks, he finds it more than mildly pleasant to abandon his irresolution about continuing his journey and to accompany Sophy to Paris as her guide and mentor. Sophy, unencumbered by the social conditioning of the upper class, is direct and naive, honest in her emotional responses. She frankly enjoys George's company, and he in turn is touched by her lack of dissimulation. Their originally innocent fling ends in several days of lovemaking. Predictably, it delights Sophy, while at the end it disgusts George both with himself and with her. It burdens him with guilt and, later, with a rationalizing self-defensiveness.

The second and third books continue to be devoted to George's story, as he becomes the increasingly prominent center of narrative consciousness. The second book brings him at last to Givré, to Anna. In her household, besides her stepson Owen, are her young daughter Effie, her mother-in-law the Marquise de Chantelle, and Sophy Viner, whom she had just engaged as a governess for Effie. Anna esteems and gets along well with her stepson Owen. She supports Owen's desire to marry Sophy, whose less-than-stable, lower middle-class background, not to mention her affair with George, is still unknown to Anna. Marriage between Owen and Sophy is opposed by the Marquise de Chantelle, not because she possesses any specific information about Sophy's unsuitability, but simply because Sophy is not a member of the social set to which the Marquise belongs. Anna, reticent by nature and social training, counters the Marquise's position in this matter in a surprisingly active way. She is prepared to wage a campaign, to take risks in behalf of Owen's suit.

George is unpleasantly surprised, to put it mildly, to find Sophy installed at Givré. The third book dwells primarily on his anguish as he strives to adapt to this uncomfortable state of affairs and to the further revelation that Sophy may well become Owen's wife. In Anna's eyes, her own marriage to George is contingent on Owen's happiness, that is, on his being able to marry Sophy. For all George's diplomatic skill at verbal fencing, his deportment toward and around Sophy is such that Owen begins intuitively to suspect something. George admits only to having known Sophy casually some years ago. Owen's intention to marry Sophy— it is not yet an engagement—is strongly opposed by George, acting out of an exquisite blend of self-interest, class consciousness, and an unquestioning assumption of a double standard of sexual morality. George can afford, however, to mute his opposition—and lessen the risk of revealing his previous intimacy with Sophy—for it is the general assumption at Givré that the Marquise de Chantelle will never permit Owen to marry a girl with an anonymous background. Surprisingly though, when a confidante to whom the Marquise has turned, approves the match, the Marquise too gives her approval. The reader does not look directly into Sophy's soul as he does into that of George, but in dialogue with the latter Sophy reveals an anguish at the situation at least as intense as George's. Moreover, her position is much more vulnerable, for she is both a woman and a member of a lower social class.

The fourth and fifth books concentrate on Anna's story, and she is the center of narrative consciousness throughout. Her misgivings about George have been awakened by Owen's intuitive suspicions. When George at last confesses his affair with Sophy, Anna, shocked back into self-doubt, proves all too ready to believe that the liaison represented a meeting of hearts as well as of sexual desires, that George is in love with Sophy. Anna, true daughter of her society, can countenance, however reluctantly, George's having sown wild oats. But she fears and dreads the possibility that he might be in love with Sophy, despite his protests to the contrary. When Sophy frankly admits having wanted the affair with George, it is almost more than Anna can bear. For it is obvious that even if George felt no love for Sophy, Sophy nevertheless was, and is, in love with him.

Sophy breaks her engagement to Owen, gives up her position as governess, and departs for Paris. Anna is torn between her love for George, her own emotional restraint, and her struggle to overcome that restraint. Anna's torment dooms George's belated efforts to patch things up with her in a rational way, one that might offer some chance of future mutual happiness. He leaves Givré.

As the fifth book begins, three days after George's goodby, Anna precipitately leaves Givré for Paris, in search of Sophy. She concludes that only Sophy can help her to regain her serenity: "[Sophy's] kept faith with herself and I haven't." Sophy's keeping faith has consisted in her breaking off with Owen and remaining away from him, a renunciation that had been insisted upon by Anna coldly and self-ishly and by George hypocritically, and that is abetted by Sophy's own sensitivity to the situation.

Anna cannot locate Sophy in Paris, for the latter has fled back to the entourage of Mrs. Murrett, her erstwhile employer, whose salon in London seems to have been outside the pale of respectability. (On this matter we take the word of George, who was an infrequent visitor, as well as that of Sophy herself.) Anna receives this information from Sophy's sister, a blowsy occasional artist who presides over a dingy hotel suite from her bed. Two disreputable male hangers-on are present when Anna calls, one of whom, it

emerges, is Sophy's former boyfriend. The ending of the
novel is thus an open one. It is true that before Anna im-
petuously follows up the lead involving Sophy's sister,
George sends word that he intends to visit Anna that same
afternoon. There is no reason to suspect that he will not do
so. Most critics seem to regard this as justifying the assumption that George and Anna will in fact marry. Such a point
of view more or less disregards the desperate tone of the
final chapter, of which the climax is Anna's interview with
Sophy's sister. But it is also true that this last chapter is not
very well integrated with the rest of the novel.

The Reef begins with a prologue—the affair of Sophy
and George—that might well constitute an independent
novella. It ends with an epilogue, the final chapter, that is
even more independent of the novel. While the body of the
novel is intrinsically connected with, and derived from, the
prologue, no such connection binds the body of the novel
with the somewhat unexpected epilogue. It is almost as
though Wharton, fearing that too much sympathy might
have accrued to Sophy, and too little to Anna, tacked on an
ending designed to right such an imbalance—and succeeded
only in destroying Anna as well.

Perhaps paradoxically, the effect of this final scene on
the modern reader's estimation of Sophy is far from all bad.
Wharton's sympathy with Sophy, lively enough during the
latter's idyll with George in Paris, is quite markedly withdrawn when Sophy's aspirations to better herself bring her to
the—for her—alien environment of Givré. The final deni-
gration of Sophy in the last chapter, on the basis of her
sordid social origins and the company she used to keep, is
cruel and gratuitous, and, perhaps because of the latter,
clumsy as well. The overkill may well induce the modern
reader to sympathize with Sophy all the more because she
has the integrity to emerge from such an environment as an
honest, attractive person. Unaffected and forthright, un-
versed in the dissembling and the one-upmanship of the

society she now finds herself in, she instinctively tells the
truth, however painful for herself. Sophy gives generously of
herself, whether as Effie's governess or as George's lover. It
is her misfortune that the man's reciprocal generosity falls
far short of the child's.

Owen Leath, Anna's stepson, differs from his elders at
Givré in his honest emotionality, which is partly, but not
entirely, a reflection of his youthfulness. He is enough of an
iconoclast in his society to share with Sophy such traits as
forthrightness and an aversion to dissembling and deviousness. The reader, sensing this essential harmony of outlook
between the two, is at first distressed that their marriage is
prevented. Later, the reader is perhaps even disappointed
when it emerges that Sophy is in love with George and so,
reacting honestly, declines to marry Owen. Owen's reaction
in turn is incredulousness, anger, and then flight. At the end
of the novel, he is on a train for Spain, and we are sorry for
him.

The Marquise de Chantelle, Anna's mother-in-law,
Owen's grandmother, is the *eminence grise* at Givré. The
decision about Owen's marriage to Sophy is ultimately hers
to make—and she proves amazingly susceptible to the
affirmative advice of her own friend, another expatriate
American, Adelaide Painter. For despite the Marquise de
Chantelle's melodious French name—one thinks of *chanter*
"to sing"—it is simply a legacy of her second marriage,
along with a conversion to Catholicism. She is as much—or
as little—an American as the rest, and her connections with
French society are just as tenuous. Despite having lived in
France since she was twenty, she does not hesitate to give
querulous vent to her detestation of French mores, especially
those that sanction a less than inhibited relationship between
the sexes.

Sophy emerged from a sordid environment to be the
admirable person she is—and this comes through despite
Wharton's withdrawal of sympathetic depiction after the

first book. What are we then to think about Anna? Anna, despite having been endowed with what is traditionally viewed as a privileged upbringing, does not behave with integrity either toward herself or toward others. Still, if we think of "the reef" in the title of the novel as suggesting Anna's personal plight, we must add the important qualification that she is at least not immobile on this reef. She is a victim of an overly repressive, highly artificial social system. Under the impetus of belated love (her late husband, Fraser Leath, practically personified their passionless society), she breaks free only with difficulty and only under the most favorable conditions, to face realities. She is not, in other words, to be charged with total failure.

In the course of the novel she has been progressing painfully away from emotional inhibition and restraint and toward greater emotional freedom. George attributes to Anna a great deal of what he calls "measure." In Wharton's words, "[Anna] was not used to strong or full emotions. . . ." The concluding clause of this sentence, however, is just as significant as the first: ". . . but she had always known that she should not be afraid of them." (In Wharton's English we are to understand "should" as the equivalent of "would.") Feeling is not something Anna fears, at least not now. As Nevius puts the matter, her "ideal of duty gradually succumbs to her passion for Darrow. . . ."

Anna's continuing contact with George Darrow is reflected by increasing emotional freedom; absences from Darrow are reflected, on the whole, by return to the inhibitory pattern. The thrust of the novel is in the form of a zigzag between these poles; it is difficult to avoid the conclusion that Anna's is a wavering character. Even such a master of character oscillation as Henry James seems baffled by Anna: "I'm not sure that her oscillations are not beyond our notation"—that is, beyond our ability to explain systematically and logically. Perhaps these oscillations reflect a certain ambivalence on the part of Wharton, who seems none-

theless to approve of Anna's sensibilities on the whole. But
Anna's penultimate change of course, her flight to Paris to
try to find Sophy, has a most ironic effect. For all her
kindness to Sophy at Givré, Anna regarded the girl at that
time as incapable of possessing very much moral sensitivity.
But now in her own crisis it is Sophy she seeks out. "It was
Sophy Viner only who could save her—Sophy Viner only
who could give her back her serenity." Anna's final oscillation to a state of horror at the environment of Sophy's sister
does nothing to restore her to our esteem, for she is declar-
ing Sophy guilty by—past—association.

George is probably able to recognize "measure" in
Anna because he shares, though to a lesser extent, the same
trait. That aside, it is difficult for the modern reader to find
much to admire in him. A dilettante, perhaps in life as well
as at his profession, he strikes us as priggish and sanctimoni-
ous. An affair with a vital girl like Sophy might have somehow contributed to humanizing him, at least as a start. When
it only releases self-disgust and guilt, George ceases to be
sympathetic to the modern reader. Thus the reader is not
likely to identify with him in his courtship of Anna.

George turns out to be only too willing to make Sophy
a victim of the double standard in order to save his own
skin, shifting the blame for the affair onto her. Given both
Sophy's pragmatic prudence and her defenselessness, the
reader is apt to think that the interests of all the characters
at Givré—not to mention the "moral sensitivity" we have
been hearing about—would be better served if George simply kept quiet. And when it becomes clear that Sophy is in
love with him, while he is not in love with her, his behavior
takes on an even less appealing light.

Since Wharton was usually highly sensitive to the tragic
consequences of the double standard, and not infrequently
angry about them, her treatment of the subject in *The Reef*
is disappointing. Silence toward it would be bad enough,

but she went so far as to offer a rationalized and inhumane
defense of the standard. She clearly felt that Sophy got her
just deserts. This serves to underline the fact that the most
important denominator of Wharton's concerns and assumptions is not the factor of sexual discrimination, as reflected
in the double standard, but the factor of social class. Lily
Bart in *The House of Mirth,* a *déclassée* upper-class girl, in
her confrontation with the double standard, is accorded
authorial sympathy; Sophy Viner, a hoyden of lower middle-
class origins, is not.

Louis Auchincloss has suggested that "The Château,"
i.e., Givré, would be a more appropriate title for *The Reef.*
But there is no deeper reason—Wharton's almost professional interest in French architecture aside—that would
warrant any such retitling, and Auchincloss is careful to stay
clear of the older critical consensus that the château exerted
a pervasive force on its inhabitants and its visitors. Wharton
dwells lovingly and appreciatively on the "lustrous greyish-
purple slates of the roof," the escutcheoned piers, "the
domed chapel terminating one of the wings," as well as on
the grassy court filled with linden trees and rectangular
yews. However, these and other such generously described
details, authentically French as they undoubtedly are, do not
mask our perception of the essential nonrelationship of
Givré to its neighborhood. Givré could be anywhere.

In the same way that Givré lacks connection with its
ambience, the people within the château are largely unre-
lated to Givré. At the most, Givré stands as a symbol of
what is old and traditional. It is a correctly, even exquisitely,
decorated stage on which the characters play out their roles.
Anna does not in the least mind the prospect of leaving
Givré. Owen does not want to inherit it. George muses at its
splendor, but there is little interaction between him and the
château. Only Sophy, the outsider, seems to be emotionally
affected by Givré. Vivacious and adventuresome in Paris,

she is frightened, cautious, and unhappy at the château—
and even in her case it seems likely that the change in her
personal situation plays a larger role in her change of outlook than does Givré.

Henry James was surely the first to point out what he
called the "unreferred" connection between the *mise-en-
scène* and the characters. But he does not hesitate to justify
Givré solely on the basis of Wharton's beautiful descriptions
of it. In general, James was enthusiastic about *The Reef*.
After receiving a copy sent him by Wharton he voiced his
appreciation of the work to her in a long letter from Lamb
House dated December 4 and 9, 1912. He mentions "the
entire interest and charm, the supreme validity and distinction," of *The Reef*. He describes "the impression of its quality" on him, and calls it "quite the finest thing you have
done; both *more* done than even the best of your other
doing, and more worth it, through intrinsic value, interest
and beauty."

Despite his generally enthusiastic approval, however,
James did not fail to note what he regarded as difficulties,
for example, his difficulty in "notating" Anna's "oscillations."
He worries a bit about the change in narrative consciousness in mid-novel, from that of George to that of Anna, as
well as about the "unreferred" nature of the characters and
the milieu. But again, overall, he perceives its superior
dramatic nature and, indeed, its "psychologic Racinian
unity."

It is probable that at least three factors lie at the root of
the former critical view that Wharton was a literary disciple
of James: the presumed Jamesian tone of *The Reef*, James's
laudatory criticism of *The Reef*, and the friendship between
Wharton and James. The latter two are facts, although that
does not in either case guarantee literary influence. But in
the case of *The Reef*, the Jamesian influence is not so much
in style as in the setting of the novel, in its characters, and in
its internal balance. Wharton's own style, increasingly ironic

and subtle, by no means excluding the plain word, bears very little resemblance to James's complex and qualified periods. As to the Jamesian setting and somewhat Jamesian characters, it is interesting to speculate to what extent they may have contributed to dulling the livelier social sensibilities that Wharton reveals in her earlier novels.

6

∽ᓀ∽ᓀ∽ᓀ∽ᓀ∽ᓀ∽ᓀ∽ᓀ∽ᓀ∽ᓀ∽ᓀ∽ᓀ∽ᓀ∽ᓀ∽ᓀ∽ᓀ∽

Ethan Frome

In a time of despair over her husband and her marriage, over her relationship to Walter Berry and her love affair with Morton Fullerton, Edith Wharton wrote—or rewrote—*Ethan Frome* (1911). The first, fragmentary version, a few pages in French, she had written some four years previously as practice material for private lessons in French that she was taking in Paris. Having lost the copybook in which she had written the fragment, she apparently started the story afresh, in English, about a year later and worked on it over the next two or three years. The final version, although it deals with poor and simple people in the Massachusetts back country, is a crucible into which she poured, as R. W. B. Lewis declares, "deep and intense private emotions." Whether it is her best novel or not, it is quite likely her best known—although she could not see why. And it certainly marks a turning point in her career as a writer, in that from then on her own strongest feelings were to go into her fiction rather than her poetry.

Ethan Frome is a frame story. It is ostensibly related by an engineer, whom we may guess to be in his thirties, after he had obtained the story in bits and pieces during an enforced stay in late winter in the village of Starkfield. (The stay is caused by a strike. Are Wharton's patrician sympathies with the striking carpenters? Rare for her time, she issues no invectives against strikes, which were in those days commonly thought to be criminal.) The narrator is "pulled up sharp" by the most impressive figure in Starkfield, though the latter "was but the ruin of a man," lame, bleak, and seemingly unapproachable. Ethan Frome has looked and acted thus ever since his sled crashed twenty-four years ago.

Ethan and his wife Zenobia already seem old at the time of the events in the story; we learn with some surprise that they are, respectively, twenty-eight and thirty-four. Seven years before the story starts, Ethan married his cousin Zenobia Pierce, who had come over from the next valley to help nurse Ethan's mother through her last illness. Zenobia, called Zeena, developed hypochondria. Again, as it seemingly was before her nursing stint, it is her chief preoccupation. This, added to her disinclination to accept any change, causes Ethan's hope of selling his run-down farm and trying his luck in a city to go aglimmering. (He had studied a year at a technological college in Worcester and had worked in Florida and thus knew something of the world he wanted to live in.)

On the recommendation of one of her several doctors that she look for someone to assist her with the housework, Zeena arranges for Mattie Silver, daughter of one of her cousins, to take the job of an unpaid servant, whom she can abuse with virtual impunity. Mattie's frailness gives Zeena more than ample opportunity for such abuse. A mutual attraction develops between Mattie and Ethan, already beaten down by Zeena's harshness and pretended ill-health; their happiness consists of inarticulate flashes of rapport. Only months later, on a night when Zeena is in another village to see yet another doctor, in pursuit of yet another cure, is Ethan emboldened to make his first amorous advances to Mattie, circumspectly and awkwardly, in the hope of a kiss or a light caress. (His thoughts are a good deal bolder, dwelling on what his life might be like if Zeena were dead.) The warmth of the evening is brought to an apprehensive end by the accidental breaking of one of Zeena's

sacred, never-used pickle dishes. That the pickle dish, a
wedding gift, has never been used makes it a strong symbol
of Zeena herself, who prefers not to take part in life. The
depth of Zeena's reaction to its being broken is revealed by
her angrily twitching lips and by "two small tears . . . on her
lashless lids."

Meanwhile, Zeena has acquired the medical recommendation that she hire a housekeeper because she is too ill
to do any of the housework. Although in fact, since the
arrival of Mattie, Zeena has done very little housework, such
a recommendation is most welcome because it provides her
with an excuse to get rid of Mattie, of whom she has become
increasingly jealous. Zeena declares that, having "given"
Mattie a job for a year, she has no more responsibility for
the girl. Mattie is to leave the very next day, the same day
on which her already-hired replacement is to arrive. Although Zeena has arranged for the handy man to drive
Mattie to the railroad station, Ethan angrily declares his
own intention of doing so. And he does.

Only on this last drive does the rapport between Ethan
and Mattie—it has now become mutual passion—cease to
be primarily inarticulate. Articulateness begins when the
thoughts of each turn to nearby Shadow Pond, where the
previous summer, at a picnic, they had first become aware of
their love for each other. Now, in winter, they revisit
Shadow Pond on the way to the station. Realizing that Mattie will likely marry someone else, Ethan avers that he would
rather have her dead than married to someone else. "Oh, I
wish I was!" Mattie sobs.

This first outbreak of despair is, however, suppressed
for the time being. Inspired by the sight of two boys coasting, a sight that reminds them of Ethan's unfulfilled promise
to take Mattie coasting, they now coast, for the fun and the
thrill, and to postpone the moment of leave-taking. As they
walk back up the hill, with the intention of leaving the
borrowed sled where they found it, they embrace passion-

ately. The hopelessness of their love is borne in on them more strongly than ever. They must stay together. But the only way they can do that is in death.

Mattie is the one who actually proposes suicide. They take off again in the sled, flying down the slope. Ethan's intent is to steer a collision course into a big elm tree in the center of the coast. But as he brushes aside a vision of Zeena's face between him and his target, he swerves the sled. Despite Ethan's instant redirection, that swerve results in an imperfect collision. Though injured, Mattie and Ethan survive. At the time of the fictive narrator's visit to Starkfield, they have been living for at least twenty-four years after the smash-up, as cripples, under the care and dominance of Zeena.

That we are shocked by the apparent changes in Ethan, Mattie, and Zeena is a measure of Wharton's powerful writing, for we are persuaded of the inevitability, even as we are shocked. Zeena now takes care of both Ethan and the more seriously injured Mattie, while before the accident she was unable even to take care of herself. Mattie, who before the accident was vivacious and sweet, is now immobile and querulous. Though the Ethan of the central story was prematurely old, his taciturnity and shyness were in fact gradually disappearing, his emotions were coming to life, in the presence of Mattie. But now he is a ruin of a man, and "there is something bleak and unapproachable in his face." He is assigned to the living dead by the local informant who says, ". . . if she'd [Mattie] ha' died, Ethan might ha' lived." This is an ironic reversal of the situation before the accident, when Ethan only began to live by virtue of the presence and influence of Mattie. But in the long years after the accident, the continued presence of Mattie in the household could only contribute further to Ethan's grief.

The fifty-two-year-old Ethan, despite his added misery, his suffering when Zeena and Mattie "get going at each other," and his face that would break one's heart, is not now essentially different from what he was in the first years of his marriage. Even then he had an immense tolerance for suffering (like Edith Wharton); even then he was capable of cheerfulness and a close personal relationship with a responsive person, that is, Mattie. Now his tolerance for suffering has been tested longer; now he is still capable, though with greater difficulty, of sympathetic human interaction with an interested person, that is, the fictive narrator.

The distance between Ethan and the narrator is at first only "bridged for a moment." It is bridged for a longer period when Ethan finds the narrator's lost book on biochemistry and agrees he would like to borrow it. Then Ethan volunteers to drive the narrator through a snowstorm to enable him to keep an appointment. And finally, the ultimate gesture of friendliness and openness: on the return trip Ethan invites the narrator to spend the stormy night in his house. As we know, it is not a happy house, and a less sympathetic man than Ethan Frome would hardly have risked exposing its spiritual and material impoverishment to a virtual stranger. To be sure, the narrator is probably the only stranger in twenty years to set foot in the house. But our point is: Ethan remains, in all his misery, capable of reacting in a friendly and sympathetic way.

Zeena, as we see her ill-naturedly ministering to the needs of the invalid Mattie and the partial cripple Ethan, is a replica of the Zeena who nursed Ethan's mother thirty-two years ago. And both Zeenas, the early and the recent, are consistent with the intervening hypochondriac Zeena, who was preoccupied with nursing herself. Wharton implies a still earlier hypochondriac stage, as she insists on the relationship of the nurse with the hypochondriac, which is in fact psychologically valid: ". . . her [early] skill as a nurse had been acquired by the absorbed observation of her own symptoms."

Mattie's personality is the only one that has basically changed. When Mattie, the outsider, arrived in Starkfield, she was vital and light-hearted in a community typified by, and given to, "deadness." Mattie wore bright red ribbons in her hair in a locale characterized by a "sky of iron," by ice, snow, gray, and black. However inevitably, however innocently, Mattie became the third point in a domestic triangle. However agreeable her disposition, Mattie was a threat to the Fromes' marriage, and Zeena knew it. Finally, Mattie had to live, or half-live, with the realization that only as a hopeless cripple was she acceptable under Zeena's roof. (Of course Zeena took her back when Mattie was no longer a threat, and when her presence could only make Ethan's life more miserable.)

Mattie must now contend with Zeena's meanness at close range—only on summer days can Mattie be moved out of the house for a few hours. In short, Mattie's is a ruined life in every way, and she is compelled to reexperience that ruin every day of her life in the house with Ethan and Zeena.

As the characterizations are complex, free of cliché, believable, and even gripping, Edith Wharton's best characters yet, so the style of *Ethan Frome* is her best yet— perhaps best ever—taut, precise, unpretentious. Realism is suggested by leitmotiv: "deadness," "sky of iron," rather than by lists of details. Wharton refrained from moralizing, and from pointing out the theme. And that theme must be simply: tragedy. Some people—Ethan Frome and Mattie above all, but also Zeena—are fated for suffering.

Gradations of morality play no role and are probably irrelevant critical impositions on the novel. Ethan and Mattie sin against certain moral codes in their illicit but hardly profligate passion and in their willingness to commit suicide. Zeena does not break these codes; but Zeena fails the test of humaneness.

The morality of Starkfield as a whole is not even alluded to, but there is generous mention of the suffering of Starkfield's inhabitants. The unhappy fact of being fated for suffering makes itself known well before fate itself descends. And nothing can be done, either early or late, to avert it— witness the appearance of Zeena's face before Ethan's eyes, between the speeding sled and its target, the elm tree. That the face is a manifestation of Ethan's mental state only underscores the fated nature of the outcome.

There is a persuasive parallel between Wharton's tormented life at this period and the tormented life of Ethan Frome. Despite her declaration that her characters always "arrived" in her novels bearing their own names, the fact is that Ethan Frome did not have that name in earlier versions of the story. He attained his final name only after Wharton's intense personalization of the original story idea. This was possibly a consequence of Wharton's despair over her unrequited love for Walter Berry, but more likely a consequence of the end of her affair with Morton Fullerton.

Parallels between Wharton's circumstance and that of Ethan come readily to mind. Both are trapped in hopeless marriages to uncongenial spouses. Both are married to spouses of uncertain health, who are, moreover, given to excessive contemplation of their states of ill health, real and imagined. Both spouses—Teddy Wharton and Zeena Frome —incline at various times and in varying degrees to irrationality. Both Edith Wharton and Ethan Frome are drawn to sweethearts more congenial than their spouses, but in each case marriage to these sweethearts cannot be achieved. Ethan even considers fleeing to the west with Mattie, but cannot, owing both to poverty and to conscience, any more than Edith could flout her society by fleeing to Egypt with Walter Berry (who helped her a good deal in the writing of *Ethan Frome*) or by establishing a permanent liaison with Morton Fullerton.

Of course these parallels are broad and basic. Perhaps for that reason they are the more convincing. Wharton may not have been aware that she was writing about herself. This hypothesis has the advantage of offering an explanation, more intrinsic than those based on locale or structure, of why *Ethan Frome* is regarded—correctly—as somehow "different" from her other works. It may perhaps even explain why, throughout the years—beginning in the 1930s—*Ethan Frome* has been the most read and best liked of Wharton's novels, despite her own misgivings about its primacy.

The misgivings become merely mild reservations by the time *Ethan Frome* was dramatized by Owen and Donald Davis in 1935, when Wharton was seventy-three. She goes on, in the course of a brief foreword to the drama, to laud highly the work of the Davises: ". . . few [novelists] have had the luck to see the characters they had imagined in fiction transported to the stage without loss or alteration of any sort, without even the grimacing enlargement of gesture and language supposed to be necessary to 'carry' over the footlights."

Besides the restraint and skill of the Davises, two qualities of Wharton's original work contribute greatly to a successful dramatization. First, the structure: the expository frame at the beginning and end provides a largely expository prologue and moving epilogue to the drama contained between. Second, Wharton's complex and thoroughly believable characterizations: Owen Davis had no use for simple characterizations and evidently reacted with enthusiasm to the dramatic possibilities in Mattie, Zeena, and Ethan. After a Philadelphia opening, the play enjoyed a run of more than four months at the National Theater in New York City before going on the road, a commercial as well as a critical success. Ruth Gordon played Mattie, Pauline Lord played Zeena, and Raymond Massey was Ethan, to the applause of audiences and the praise of drama critics.

The original novel began to attain something like its present popularity only in the 1930s—some twenty and more years after Wharton wrote it. Conventional wisdom has it that the great depression provided a readership receptive to the realistic milieu of *Ethan Frome.* That seems a dubious logic; we may prefer to think that the drama played no small role in establishing the novel as a classic by bringing its characterizational as well as its descriptive merits to the attention of a wider circle of influential readers.

7

੭੭ੑੑੑੑੑੑੑੑੑੑੑੑੑੑੑੑੑੑੑੑੑੑੑੑੑੑੑੑ

The Short Stories

Beginning with "Mrs. Manstey's View," which was first published in *Scribner's Magazine*, July 1891, and ending with "All Souls," apparently written a year or so before her death in 1937, Wharton wrote eighty-six short stories in all. Most of them dwell on the foibles of the New York society —and its European extension—with which she was most familiar. Even the ghost stories among them generally take place within the familiar social precincts.

"Mrs. Manstey's View" is exceptional, although not unique. It is a realistic story whose characters are members of the lower middle class. Mrs. Manstey, seventeen years a widow, lives in a third-floor back room of a New York boarding house. She has few friends. At one time she dreamed of living in the country; the residue of that dream is a vague tenderness for animals and plants—more tenderness, it must be owned, than she has for people. The most important thing in her life is the view from her window. Consisting chiefly of adjacent backyards, it is hardly a beautiful view, although it does include the spire of a distant brownstone church and even a far-off factory chimney. Directly beneath her window is an ailanthus tree. In the next yard is a magnolia, further off a horse chestnut, wisteria, and syringa.

When one April day Mrs. Manstey's landlady informs her that the adjoining house is going to be enlarged, Mrs.

Manstey realizes that her all-important view is going to be obliterated by brick and mortar. She is too old, her routine is too set, for her to contemplate moving. She goes to call on the owner of the adjacent house, Mrs. Black, and emotionally offers her a thousand dollars—half of her wealth—to cancel the proposed construction. Thinking her mad, Mrs. Black promises to consider the offer. But next morning Mrs. Manstey hears the workmen below in the yard. Depressed, she does not get up until the afternoon, when she goes to take her familiar seat at the window. As she sadly surveys the preliminary construction work, she hears one workman tell another not to throw matches near the barrels of paper and rubbish under the balcony.

That night a spring storm disturbs Mrs. Manstey's sleep. Throwing on a thin dressing gown, she takes from her closet the kettle of kerosene used for lamps, slips some matches into her pocket, descends four stories into the basement, opens the basement door, and in a gust of cold wind gropes her way out into the yard. When a fire alarm at three in the morning brings all the boarders to their windows, Mrs. Manstey is among them, still in her thin dressing gown.

The fire destroys only the back balcony of Mrs. Black's house. But Mrs. Manstey has caught pneumonia, and her condition rapidly becomes critical. At her barely audible request, her landlady and her nurse lift her to her chair by the window. It is a beautiful spring dawn. The brownstone spire shines golden. The magnolia has unfolded more flowers. The charred sections of Mrs. Black's balcony lie on the ground. Smiling, Mrs. Manstey dies. That day the construction resumes.

Far different from "Mrs. Manstey's View," and more familiar to Wharton's readers in social milieu, is "The Pelican," which was first published in *Scribner's Magazine*, November 1898. A young widow with a six-month-old son, Mrs. Amyot becomes a professional lecturer. In those days, we are told, it was a simple matter to put together a passable lecture from what one could glean in a library reading room. This is fortunate for Mrs. Amyot, for she is rather simple-minded, and her memory is far from good. She is, however, extraordinarily facile with words. Her audiences are not too demanding, so Mrs. Amyot does well on the lecture circuit. She continually lets it be understood that she is "doing it for the baby."

Mrs. Amyot's fame grows. In fashionable circles it is now a duty to be seen at her lectures—never mind that they are still devoid of intellectual content. And now she repeatedly contrives to let it be known that she is doing it so as to be able to afford a good education for her son Lancelot. He has been sent to the best schools possible and is soon to enter Harvard. But by the time Lancelot is in Harvard, lecture audiences have become more discriminating, so that Mrs. Amyot is less in demand.

Ten years pass since Mrs. Amyot's fortunes began to decline. The narrator, evidently a male professor, is spending some time at a southern health resort. By chance, Mrs. Amyot is scheduled to give a lecture there, and sure enough, the word goes around that she lectures to pay for her son's education. This is heard not only by the narrator, but also by a brown-bearded man a little past thirty. The latter insists on taking the narrator, a self-confessed "old friend" of Mrs. Amyot, to meet her after the lecture.

The brown-bearded man—he is, as we have guessed, Lancelot Amyot, who has come, at his mother's invitation, clear from Minneapolis to hear her lecture—further insists that his mother declare the truth in the presence of her old friend: has she been saying she gives lectures to pay for his, Lancelot's, education?

Lancelot's pride is at stake. He has supported his wife and children for almost ten years and has paid his mother back every cent she spent on his education. Why does she continue to lie? When her son abruptly departs after this embarrassing scene, Mrs. Amyot shows no resentment. Rather, with tears running down her cheeks, she proclaims that she sent her son's wife a sealskin jacket at Christmas.

"The Other Two," according to R. W. B. Lewis, is "the most nearly perfect short story Edith Wharton ever wrote." It first appeared in *The Descent of Man and Other Stories* (1904). Waythorn—our continuing ignorance of his first name contributes to our eventual sense of his unimportance —has just become the third husband of the former Mrs. Alice Varick, who previously had been Mrs. Alice Haskett. New York City society knew nothing of Alice's first husband Mr. Haskett and so believed the worst of him. Alice's second marriage, to Gus Varick, "was a passport to the set whose recognition she coveted." The Varicks were a popular couple for a few years, but Gus's adulteries eventually led to Alice's second divorce.

Mr. and Mrs. Waythorn are recalled from their honeymoon by the illness of Lily Haskett, Alice's twelve-year-old child. Upon Alice's first divorce the court had given Haskett the right to visit his daughter, as well as the right to be consulted on matters concerning her welfare. Until Lily fell ill, the visits took place at his boarding house—he had taken a less rewarding job to move to New York City to be near Lily. Now that Lily is immobilized by illness, he wishes to exercise his right to visit her at the Waythorns. Waythorn reluctantly agrees, and contrives to stay away from home on visiting day until well after the visiting hour.

Meanwhile, the illness of Waythorn's business partner forces Waythorn into a close business relationship with a new client of the firm, Gus Varick. Waythorn returns home after his conference with Varick, and Haskett fortunately has departed. After dinner, Alice pours him some coffee, then adds to it a liqueur glass of cognac. Waythorn protests that he does not take cognac in his coffee. When their eyes meet, Alice blushes in agony.

As his relationship with Varick grows closer, Waythorn

begins to have insights into his wife's past; he recognizes in her the gift of adaptability to first one man, then another. And now he meets Haskett, who is legally empowered to consult with him in the case of what he believes to be an unsuitable governess for Lily. Upon finding Haskett most reasonable and unprepossessing, Waythorn comes to a still more complete understanding of Alice. He sees that she took her change of husbands like a change of weather. "He held so many shares in his wife's personality, and his predecessors were his partners in the business."

One afternoon Waythorn finds Haskett in the library waiting for Alice, with whom he has an appointment to discuss Lily—now recovered from her illness. After Waythorn offers Haskett a cigar, the door opens and Varick enters, having missed Waythorn downtown. Embarrassments are relieved somewhat when a footman comes in carrying a tea table. Waythorn offers Varick a cigar. Alice enters, fresh and smiling, late but unperturbed. She sees Varick first, then Haskett, shakes hands with each, and suggests they all have tea before talking business. The two visitors advance to receive the cups she holds out to them. "She glanced about for Waythorn, and he took the third cup with a laugh." The reader understands that Waythorn has completely accepted his fractional role in Alice's life. Thus Wharton has observed the inevitable result of successive marriages, as well as man's, and woman's, adaptability as partners in such marriages.

"The Last Asset," which appeared in *Scribner's Magazine* in August 1904, takes place in Paris. The principal characters are expatriate Americans, including the fictive narrator, a young journalist named Garnett who not only narrates, but also plays a key role in the story. Over the past two years, he has become somewhat acquainted with a fellow diner in a restaurant they both frequent, an old gentleman given to expounding his philosophy of life. This philosophy consists primarily of trying to get one's life down

to routine and eliminating the possibility of surprise. It occurs to Garnett that he and his gently garrulous acquaintance have exchanged views on life for two years and
still do not even know each other's names.

Garnett receives a note from a Mrs. Sam Newell, announcing her arrival at the Ritz and her need to see him
immediately. He knows she is at the point of losing her
position in international society, that she is falling in with
very undesirable people in her effort to revive her social
fortunes. He cannot imagine why she should have need of
him. He soon finds out.

Mrs. Newell's daughter Hermione is to be married to
the Comte Louis du Trayas, a member of one of the most
distinguished families of France. Such an alliance will restore Mrs. Newell's social position. Hermione herself is an
exceptionally sweet and innocent girl, deeply in love with
her fiance, as he is with her. The problem: the Trayas family, having sanctioned the match reluctantly, will withdraw
their sanction unless the bride's father, in accord with
French custom, accompanies the bride at the wedding. Mrs.
Newell, however, discarded her husband long ago, when he
ceased to be useful to her social climbing. But she had not
divorced him, for all along she had the feeling he might
someday prove useful again. Now she wishes Garnett, who
has many contacts in Paris, to search him out and persuade
him to play his part in Hermione's wedding.

Garnett discovers that Newell is living on the rue
Panonceaux, an obscure and run-down street that Garnett
has never heard of. When he confides his problem to his
philosopher-acquaintance, the latter declares that he is in
fact Samuel C. Newell. But he refuses to commit himself to
play his assigned part at the wedding; such is his distaste for
his wife and her life style. He himself, once prosperous, is
poor because he prefers to be poor. He cannot afford a
dowry—which, in any case, is being supplied by his wife's
disreputable sponsors of the moment. He can, however,

afford to be at the wedding, but demands a day to think it over.

Garnett is of two minds about his own role in trying to persuade Newell to lend himself to his wife's project, that is, Hermione's wedding. (Newell's indispensability to the project makes him "the last asset.") But Garnett is so struck by Hermione's purity and love, so aware that she may end up being corrupted by her mother if she does not escape the maternal roof, that he resolves to apply all his persuasiveness when he meets Newell the next day. And Newell does agree, for the sake of his daughter, and in perfect awareness that one way or another his wife always gets what she wants.

"The Blond Beast" first appeared in the collection, *Tales of Men and Ghosts* (1910). That Wharton's title is borrowed from a phrase coined by Nietzsche is not by chance. As early as 1908 Wharton was enthusiastically familiar with Nietzsche's *Beyond Good and Evil* and *A Genealogy of Morals*. Wharton's "blond beast"—never so called in the story—is Hugh Milner, just out of college. While there, in accordance with Nietzsche's recommendations, "he had hunted the hypothetical 'moral sense' to its lair," and had "dragged from their concealment the various self-advancing sentiments dissembled under it." Hugh, too, believes that "pity for suffering is one of the most elementary stages of egotism."

Hugh becomes first the private secretary, then the confidant of the millionaire businessman Orlando Spence. In this role he dominates the hypocritical Orlando as well as the latter's idealistic son, Draper. Hugh's health and strength, as well as his mental superiority, are duly emphasized. He, as the superman, is entitled to do what he will to secure his own dominance. There are, however, chinks in Hugh's Nietzschean superiority. A crucial sign of imperfection is his attitude toward a hurt dog. Of course, as a Nietzschean, Hugh prefers that animals "should be healthy and handsome," which the fugitive dog cringing against him is not.

Besides, the dog shows "an injudicious mingling of races" as well as "a congenital weakness of character." Limping severely, it probably will not survive the night.

The unfortunate dog, lame and bleeding, plunges desperately into a dirty snow bank and cowers in fear of two pursuing boys. Hugh, after making sure there is no one to see him acting mercifully, goes to help the dog. As he does so, he reflects that pity, one of the most primitive forms of egotism, is also one of the most tenacious. He himself has not transcended that primitive stage, which he, along with Nietzsche, believes must be transcended if man is to affirm life and represent the maximum of purity and self-mastery.

Orlando is worried about what people will say of his son's ceasing to teach a Bible class just as he, Orlando, has endowed the Orlando G. Spence College for Missionaries. He cannot understand an act based on principle—in this case, Draper's doubts about the definition of good. He bribes Hugh to speak to Draper about the Bible class. Meanwhile Orlando is beset by a newspaper investigation of his failure to sell his stock in his São Paulo plantations, as he claimed to have done at the time he was publicly denouncing the abuses visited upon the peons. Instead, he merely transferred the stock to a dummy and kept drawing his forty per cent interest. Draper, upon coming into possession of an incriminating letter in the affair, is crushed. Hugh assures Draper that the information is false and that his father, moreover, does not consider his giving up his Bible class as a form of criticism. Draper, penitent, renounces his previous doubts about his father's sincerity in seeing no conflict between his business methods and his religion.

Hugh's Nietzschean convictions are not strong enough for this second attack on them. After consciously glorying in his control of the two Spences, as well as of the situation, he resigns his position and returns the bribe to Orlando. Orlando is safe from being misunderstood, but Hugh cannot take money for making him so. Orlando: "What other guarantee have I got?" Hugh: "You've got Draper!" This seems a weak ending; Wharton herself admitted that all in all she did not bring her Nietzschean story off very satisfactorily.

"Xingu" appeared initially in *Scribner's Magazine* of December 1911. The Lunch Club in Hillbridge (probably Wharton's code for Cambridge) is composed of several "ladies who pursue Culture in bands, as though it were dangerous to meet alone . . . indomitable huntresses of erudition." The club has one member who does not fit in, Mrs. Roby. Once, upon hearing mention of the pterodactyl, Mrs. Roby had professed ignorance of poetic meters. Subsequently, Mrs. Roby sits by in typical silence while the rest of the members make fools of themselves trying to impress their guest of honor, the novelist Osric Dane. The hostess, Mrs. Ballinger, tries to excuse the members' critical incompetence by saying that they have been pursuing many serious topics, that they have recently "been so intensely interested in ——." At this Mrs. Roby prompts, "in Xingu?"

Since none of the members knows what Xingu is, they all dissemble revealingly as Mrs. Roby drops hints that it is deep, long, hard to penetrate, has many branches, and further, that one of Osric Dane's most recent books is saturated with it. During the confusion Osric Dane remembers another appointment in order to escape with Mrs. Roby and ask about Xingu. The remaining members rack their brains further and come to the conclusion that Xingu must be a language, a book, or an obscure philosophy. Finally someone thinks to look it up in the encyclopedia. It is not under the Z's, but the X's: a river in Brazil. (And during a boating party one of Mrs. Roby's friends had thrown a copy of Osric Dane's latest novel overboard—thus the saturation!) The President of the Lunch Club (Wharton resolutely capitalizes these words) sits down to draft a letter of expulsion: "My dear Mrs. Roby ——"

"Autres Temps . . ." was first published in the *Century Magazine* in July and August 1911 under the title, "Other

Times, Other Manners," an even more precise indication of
its theme. Twenty years before the story begins, Mrs. Lidcote was ostracized from society for being a party to a
divorce. The ban is total and without termination; she has
since lived in exile in Europe, and even there she has been
made to feel its force. Upon being informed of her daughter's divorce and prompt remarriage, Mrs. Lidcote sails for
New York, for she is so much a victim of her own condemned past that she imagines Leila must be going through
what she had gone through.

On the boat Mrs. Lidcote gets some inkling that this
may not be true, that, as several people say, Leila "is doing
all right." That assessment proves abundantly and, for Mrs.
Lidcote, humiliatingly true. No one holds Leila's divorce
against her in the slightest. As Mrs. Lidcote is brought by a
cousin to a splendid country mansion, Leila and her new
husband, Wilbour, are presiding genially over a huge house
party, the purpose of which is to clinch Wilbour's appointment to a diplomatic post in Rome. It quickly becomes clear
to Mrs. Lidcote that she is being kept out of view of the
guests. After a bit of rationalizing, she recognizes the all-too-
painful reason. Her presence would damage Wilbour's
chance of appointment and, on a more general level, prove
an embarrassment to Leila and her guests. The new, more
indulgent attitude of society protects Leila from any censure
relating to her divorce. But that attitude is not extended to
apply to Mrs. Lidcote. Having been condemned in the past,
she is not eligible for forgiveness in the present.

"After Holbein" is thematically related to the seven-
teenth-century woodcuts of Hans Holbein the Younger,
based on "The Dance of Death." In this series of pictures a
skeleton, death, is depicted insinuating himself into the lives
of a variety of people, which reminds us that even in the
midst of life—not to say in our old age—we are at the
mercy of death. A macabre and bitter story, "After Holbein"
was first published in *The Saturday Evening Post*, May 5,

1928. The partners in Wharton's New York Dance of Death are Anson Warley, an aging, inveterate diner-out in society, and Mrs. Evelina Jaspar, an aged and senile heiress (probably modeled after Caroline Schermerhorn Astor, a founding member of New York society in the 1860s).

Warley, whose vitality is failing, despite his pretense that he is immune from aging, goes out to keep a dinner engagement. Although it is a bitterly cold night, he insists on walking. On the way, however, he forgets his destination. Reassuring himself that the address will shortly come to mind, he proceeds. Upon seeing the brightly lit Jaspar mansion, he concludes that that is his destination, and enters. It is lit because almost every night Mrs. Jaspar, attended by a skeleton staff of old and indulgent servants—as well as a nurse—and wearing a purple wig and her much beloved diamonds, receives nonexistent and for the most part long-deceased guests at dinner. She was actually expecting Warley.

He goes along with the charade, eating mashed potatoes served in a blue crockery dish, admiring bouquets made of folded newspapers, and drinking mineral water proclaimed to be wine. There is even conversation of sorts. When his hostess suddenly tires, he takes his departure, smiling with satisfaction at the wine and the wit he has just enjoyed. Such was society at its best. He takes one step into the icy night and collapses, having succumbed to a stroke, or, in the manner of Holbein's victims, having been visited by the figure of death.

Wharton also wrote several ghost stories, a genre which in her hands often merges into the psychological horror story. Such a story is "The Eyes," which was published in *Scribner's Magazine* of June 1910. Andrew Culwin, a supremely egotistical esthete, tells the story in which he is the principal actor. As a young man, living at his aunt's and trying to write a book, he becomes acquainted with his cousin, Alice Nowell, who is neither beautiful nor intelligent and is perfectly content to be "uninteresting." After a brief intimacy, Andrew abruptly decides to leave for Europe. When he tells Alice, her disappointment is so great that his remorse impels him to a proposal of marriage. Having thus done a good deed, that night he wakes to be confronted by a pair of horrible, red-lidded eyes staring at him from the foot of the bed. Pursued by the memory and fear of those eyes, he belatedly flees to Europe.

Three years later Andrew is living in Rome. A young man, Gilbert Noyes, appears, bearing a note of introduction from Alice Nowell. Gilbert, hugely untalented, has come to Rome to try to become a writer. He fails, but he does prove a most agreeable companion to Andrew. When it is up to Andrew to tell Gilbert he has no future as a writer, he cannot do it, since he would then lose Gilbert's companionship. That night, Andrew wakes to a confrontation with the same horrible eyes he had seen on the night he proposed to Alice Nowell, and they return to him every night for a month.

By the time Andrew finishes his story the meaning of the eyes becomes apparent to everyone present, except him. To young Phil Frenham, Andrew's current special protégé, their meaning is devastatingly apparent, and we are quite justified in regarding the relationship between the two men as potentially, or perhaps actually, homosexual.

When Andrew tries to cheer Phil up, he catches sight of his own face in a mirror. At last he recognizes the eyes, not as mere delusions owing to digestive or optical difficulties, but as the means by which he is to perceive his own monstrous egoism.

If we consider the ghost story, the Nietzschean story, and the realistic "Mrs. Manstey's View" as special cases, each of considerable merit, it becomes clear that Wharton's short stories reflect in a general way the preoccupations of most of her novels. The stories are concerned with New York society, or certainly with the members of that society, from its early heyday to its eclipse and virtual disappearance.

Her concern is perhaps very slightly affectionate, but essentially ironic. The vanity, the rigidity, the inconsistency of this society and its extended membership all receive their full measure of disapproval. She treats cultural pretentiousness with a special disdain. She makes us see the cruelty—even if it is unconscious cruelty—that accompanies the vices of her society.

Wharton's short stories are as a rule very carefully crafted. Coincidence is abundant, as in the novels, but we are prepared to accept it as necessary within the shorter scope of the story. Her allusiveness is frequent and effective. Although the subject matter may be limited and even archaic, the modern reader will need no prompting to draw parallels with more familiar modern circumstances and will be vastly entertained by Wharton's skillful and none-too-charitable spotlighting of human foibles that are not necessarily limited to a certain society or era.

8

♫♫♫♫♫♫♫♫♫♫♫♫♫♫♫♫♫♫♫♫♫

Critical and Other Writings

Although Wharton is best known as a writer of novels and short stories, she by no means limited herself to prose fiction. Poetry, at first, rather than fiction, was what she poured her emotions into. Her lyric talent may be described as competent, but lacking the requisite degree of inspiration. She wrote books on interior decorating and on landscape architecture. She wrote books, well-received in their time, about her travels in France, in Italy, and in Morocco. For American readers she interpreted France and the French people, perceptively and sympathetically. In the early 1900s she translated professionally, and wrote book reviews. Late in life she wrote an autobiography. And finally she was a literary critic; not just a writer telling how she writes (she was always chary of that), but a serious, articulate, impressively well-informed critic. She published a score of critical essays in leading journals during the period 1902–1936.

In 1925 she published a compendium of five critical essays under the title *The Writing of Fiction*. At least two of the essays, "Constructing a Novel" and "Telling a Short Story," are of primary interest to us. The former begins with a historical discussion of the novel, not perhaps original, but sensible and informative: her thesis was that the modern novel is a combination of the French novel of psychology and the English novel of manners. Both in the historical discussion and in the subsequent theoretical discussion, she

91

invoked as models of excellence: Balzac, Stendhal, Jane
Austen, Trollope, George Eliot, Meredith, Henry James,
Tolstoy, Dostoevsky, and Goethe.

Narrative, said Wharton, "should furnish the substance
of the novel"; dialogue, since it forces characters to say for
the benefit of the reader what would be silently taken for
granted in real life, should never be more than an adjunct.
She found that there are two central difficulties that a novelist must resolve. The first has to do with the verisimilitude
and control of the narrative "point of vision." Wharton's
position was that the novelist must limit himself to depicting
only what the intelligence of the character associated with
the point of vision would have noticed, and the depiction
should be in terms appropriate to the register of intelligence
of that character. The point of vision should be shifted from
one character to another as seldom as possible—we have
already noted her rather consistent application of that dic-
tum to her own writing. The second central difficulty is that
of keeping so firm a hold on the "main lines" of the characters that they emerge from the passage of time at once
modified and yet their original selves: the ideal example is
Ethan Frome. Finally, the novel must contain what Wharton called "illuminating incidents" of such imaginativeness
and of such immediacy to the tale, that the ending of the
novel is perceived as completely inevitable.

The essay on the short story also begins with a historical discussion. The short story in England and America is a
descendant of the French *nouvelle*. Ghost stories, on the
other hand, descend from Germanic and Gaelic sources. If
the writer of a ghost story or a short story has given the
reader an immediate sense of security, then improbability is
in itself no problem, for, at least in the case of the ghost
story, we all retain a shadowy memory of ancestral terrors.
But tricks and effects are not to be heaped on the reader;
economy and iteration are the keys. Curiously, as works
illustrating these qualities, she cited Eugene O'Neill's *The*

Emperor Jones and Henry James's *The Turn of the Screw*, the one a play, the other far too long to be considered a short story.

Although she asserted that "rules" in art are subject to many exceptions, she made considerable point of the standard distinctions between the novel and the short story. The former is typified by the gradual unfolding of the inner life of the characters as well as by inducing in the reader a sense of the passage of time. The short story is based on situation rather than on character—in this sense it is the descendant of the epic and the ballad. Accordingly, the effect of a short story depends in a crucial way on its form, on the way it is presented. The beginning of a short story, even more than of a novel, has to contain the germ of the whole, and the reader's attention must be gained at the very outset. As an example of an attention-getting start, she offered the line: " 'Hell,' said the Duchess as she lit her cigar," although she lamented that the effectiveness of such a line is somewhat vitiated by the increasing frequency of swearing and smoking among duchesses. After the reader's attention has been thus fixed, it is essential that the story-teller then proceed with economy and simplicity to an ending that is both adequate to the story and conceivable—not one of the standardized endings one sees affixed to any number of what she calls "machine-made magazine stories."

In 1934 Wharton published her autobiography, *A Backward Glance*—portions of it had appeared during 1933 and 1934 in *The Ladies' Home Journal* and the *Atlantic Monthly*. *A Backward Glance* is in no sense a thorough or complete autobiography. Wharton included what she wanted, and left out what she wanted. For example, she did not name Teddy Wharton, but referred to him somewhat impersonally as "my husband," and scarcely mentioned him between the time of their marriage and the time when his mental health was deteriorating. Perhaps, however, we are not justified in complaining about her failure to write the book we wish she had written. She had long guarded her privacy. She had habitually avoided the limelight of publicity. *A Backward Glance* represents a very slight concession on her part.

The first chapters treat the history of her father's family and her mother's family back to Revolutionary times, and the background and development of that New York City society into which she was born. Then, most charmingly, she related her memories of herself as a little girl growing up in that society. It was not all sugar and spice; her early conflicts with her mother seemed well-etched in her memory. As in her novels, however, she did not labor the situation, but rather caused the facts to make the point. The later chapters, from our present perspective, seem often to deal with less-than-momentous events—but then Wharton had already told us in the preface, "A First Word," that she had been obliged to make the best of her unsensational material. She professed to have been at peace with everyone, to have had no enemies. And indeed, everything does seem cheerful, unbelievably cheerful. R. W. B. Lewis's biography, *Edith Wharton*, acquaints us with the ample share of stress and unhappiness that she bore but preferred not to mention in *A Backward Glance*.

Wharton had disappointingly little to say in *A Backward Glance* about her writing. We search in vain for any appreciable amount of specific and direct insight into a given novel or short story. On the other hand, reading her memories of the life she lived, filtered as they may be, provides valuable indirect insights to her fiction, for hers was not a life style that has survived into our era.

9

Conclusion

Most of Edith Wharton's fiction, from the earliest to the latest, is a mirror of her ambivalence toward her own society. (We have to except from this statement her early ventures into realism as well as *Ethan Frome* and *Summer*, the latter a short novel of the rural lower middle class, published in 1917.) She was critical of her own society even as she felt affection for it. In her earlier works scorn dominates, although not to the complete exclusion of sympathy. As she grew older and her ties with the United States became more tenuous, reminiscent affection played a larger role.

Her attitude was also shaped by the several social categories subsumed under the term, her own society. She was generally more affectionate and indulgent toward the New York City society in which she grew up, that of the 1860s and 1870s. *The Age of Innocence* is not devoid of scorn, to be sure; perhaps no writer was better equipped to see the flaws of the society that the novel depicts, and she did not hesitate to describe what she saw. *The House of Mirth*, which dwells on the successor society, corrupted, in Wharton's view, by the Invaders, is pervaded by a more concentrated scorn.

As the corrupt society blossomed, became international, and virtually obliterated the remnants of the old and "good" society, Wharton's scorn became withering, as we see in *The Custom of the Country*. The robust society in which Undine

Spragg travels later becomes pallid and superficial. When
Wharton treated it in her magazine fiction her previous
magnificent scorn became something like querulous anger at
a world that had passed her by. *The Buccaneers* completes a
circle; she was in command of her material again, that of
her society properly speaking, and she returned to affectionate irony.

The Reef shares in this pattern of development to some
extent, for in it she satirized the second of the societies
above, the successor society, rather briskly. Anna Leath's
mother-in-law, Madame de Chantelle, and her first husband,
Fraser Leath, not to mention the stuffy George Darrow, all
are the recipients of her sting. But *The Reef* also is something apart, a novel after the manner of Henry James. It is
one of a kind in the Wharton oeuvre. It is quite inaccurate
to suggest that Wharton was a disciple of James, that she
was much under his influence. The nature and extent of
James's influence on Wharton may be summed up as follows. She was not burdened with uncritical respect for
James's works. After her first meeting with him she stated
her delight that at least he spoke more lucidly than he wrote.
She denounced the complicated way in which *The Golden
Bowl* was written. *The Sacred Fount* fared no better. In
1904 she avowed that she could not read any of his books of
the last ten years. It is instructive that in 1900 she composed
a parodistic pastiche of his current style, and it simply fell
flat. In other words, even when she was consciously trying to
imitate James's style, she was not capable of it. The fact is
that their talents, after a certain amount of common ground
was covered, ran in different directions.

The common ground consisted of the background of
family and society, and the social and moral outlook that
proceeded therefrom. This outlook was reflected not so
much in the subject of the fictional work as in the quality of
mind, the point of view of the fictive person who expressed
it. The application by both writers of the inherent tenet of

moral and social sensibility could not but result in a certain identity of method as well. Wharton explicated and simplified these matters in *The Writing of Fiction*, and she reflected them in her early stories, in which the narrative point of view or, as she says, "the point of vision," was consistently superrefined, a crucible, as it were, of sensibilities. To make this completely comprehensible in the face of contemporary values, we must, at least intellectually, accept Wharton's—as well as James's—belief that morality and refinement are inextricable, are, indeed, merely slightly different facets of the same quality.

Wharton's simplification of the Jamesian tenets in *The Writing of Fiction* provides a clue to the future nature of her fictive method when, early on, it deviated from that of James. James himself suggested that the differences between Wharton and himself came to be one of relative proximity of the writer to his detail: he, like a worm, was infinitely concerned with the minutiae of the terrain, that is, the psychological terrain, of a novel; Wharton, like an eagle (a simile he also used to describe her descents on his social and professional life), flew too high and too swiftly to be concerned with such details. From Wharton's point of view, she went to the heart of things, to what really mattered, while James obfuscated that goal with his seemingly interminable restatements, qualifications, and requalifications. She knew that his kind of art was not her kind of art. She admired James as a dear and generous friend, and he was.

Despite Wharton's professions of happiness in *A Backward Glance*, she was an unhappy human being. One even feels she was unhappy as a woman. Her society subjected women to special disadvantages; in this connection we think of the plight of Lily Bart. This society subjected a brilliant woman, like Wharton, to additional humiliation by simply not recognizing her brilliance or her literary accomplishment —those were things one did not talk about. Wharton was a feminist, however, only in a limited way. Social class was more important to her than sexual equality. She deplored the double standard as it applied to Lily Bart or Ellen Olenska; she defended it as it applied to Sophy Viner. Moreover, Wharton preferred to speak in fiction with a man's voice, to work from a fictional perspective which was male. That is, whenever she employed the device of the fictive narrator, that narrator was a male. And her narrators were in every way valid and convincing in their male perspectives.

On the whole Wharton did not deal kindly with the members of her own sex as they appeared in her fiction. Her special gifts as a writer of fiction were in the areas of plotting and style. She was not an innovator of novelistic form, but she did develop the possibilities of the traditional nineteenth-century novel as far as her virtuosity could take her, which in the cases of *The House of Mirth, Ethan Frome, The Custom of the Country*, and *The Age of Innocence* was very far indeed.

It has been frequently said that Wharton's novels consist of the trivial doings of trivial people. That is largely true. But her fictional people, with whom she was for the most part on remarkably close terms of acquaintance, were part of, acted in, and typified a society in crisis, about which there were things to be said. Wharton said them, and what she did not say she ironically implied.

There is a surge of interest in Wharton today, reflected in frequent reprinting of her works as well as in the publication of biography, interpretation, and criticism. It is a more substantial surge than that which often attends the rediscovery of a first-rate writer several decades after his or her death. The reason may lie in Wharton's particular appeal to a torn society, reflecting at once deep cynicism and muted, if occasionally effective, idealism.

It is not, however, as simple as our society being a mere copy, writ large, of Wharton's society. But we and Edith Wharton share the experience of living through a relatively rapid and perceptible social upheaval. Then, for example, materialism with its social reflections was coming in, and despite her very material comfort, she was materialism's sworn enemy. Now materialism is on the defensive; and we savor the accuracy, the bite, of Wharton's attack, perhaps admiring along the way, or perhaps not entirely grasping, her erudition. Then, there was social and sexual discrimination. There still is. Wharton supported the first, decried the second, as long as it did not impinge on the first. But she did decry, and that was something, then quite likely a lonelier role than now. Wharton had courage. We find that admirable. And if it was expressed, or implied, pointedly and with wit, we find it even more admirable.

Bibliography

I. Works by Edith Wharton

1. *Books*

Verses. Newport, R.I.: C. E. Hammett, Jr., 1878.

The Decoration of Houses (with Ogden Codman, Jr.). New York: Scribner's, 1897.

The Greater Inclination. New York: Scribner's, 1899.

The Touchstone. New York: Scribner's, 1900.

Crucial Instances. New York: Scribner's, 1901.

The Valley of Decision. 2 vols. New York: Scribner's, 1902.

The Joy of Living (Es lebe das Leben). By Hermann Sudermann. Translated by Edith Wharton. New York: Scribner's, 1902.

Sanctuary. New York: Scribner's, 1903.

The Descent of Man, and Other Stories. New York: Scribner's, 1904.

Italian Villas and Their Gardens. New York: Century, 1904.

Italian Backgrounds. New York: Scribner's, 1905.

The House of Mirth. New York: Scribner's, 1905.

Madame de Treymes. New York: Scribner's, 1907.

The Fruit of the Tree. New York: Scribner's, 1907.

A Motor-Flight through France. New York: Scribner's, 1908.

The Hermit and the Wild Woman, and Other Stories. New York: Scribner's, 1908.

Artemis to Actaeon, and Other Verse. New York: Scribner's, 1909.

Tales of Men and Ghosts. New York: Scribner's, 1910.

Ethan Frome. New York: Scribner's, 1911.

The Reef. New York: Appleton, 1912.

The Custom of the Country. New York: Scribner's, 1913.

Fighting France, from Dunkerque to Belfort. New York: Scribner's, 1915.

Xingu, and Other Stories. New York: Scribner's, 1916.

The Book of the Homeless. Edited by Edith Wharton. New York: Scribner's, 1916.

Summer. New York: Appleton, 1917.

The Marne. New York: Appleton, 1918.

French Ways and Their Meaning. New York: Appleton, 1919.

The Age of Innocence. New York: Appleton, 1920.

In Morocco. New York: Scribner's, 1920.

The Glimpses of the Moon. New York: Appleton, 1922.

A Son at the Front. New York: Scribner's, 1923.

Old New York: False Dawn, The Old Maid, The Spark, New Year's Day. 4 vols. New York: Appleton, 1924.

The Mother's Recompense. New York: Appleton, 1925.

The Writing of Fiction. New York: Scribner's, 1925.

Here and Beyond. New York: Appleton, 1926.

Twelve Poems. London: The Medici Society, 1926.

Twilight Sleep. New York: Appleton, 1927.

The Children. New York: Appleton, 1928.

Hudson River Bracketed. New York: Appleton, 1929.

Certain People. New York: Appleton, 1930.

The Gods Arrive. New York: Appleton, 1932.

Human Nature. New York: Appleton, 1933.

A Backward Glance. New York: Appleton-Century, 1934.

The World Over. New York: Appleton-Century, 1936.

Ghosts. New York: Appleton-Century, 1937.

The Buccaneers. New York: Appleton-Century, 1937.

Eternal Passion in English Poetry. Selected by Edith Wharton and Robert Norton, with the collaboration of Gaillard Lapsley. New York: Appleton-Century, 1939.

2. Anthologies

An Edith Wharton Treasury. Edited by Arthur H. Quinn. New York: Appleton-Century-Crofts, 1950.

The Best Short Stories of Edith Wharton. Edited by Wayne Andrews. New York: Scribner's, 1958.

The Edith Wharton Reader. Edited by Louis Auchincloss. New York: Scribner's, 1965.

The Collected Short Stories of Edith Wharton. Edited by R. W. B. Lewis. 2 vols. New York: Scribner's, 1968.

3. *Short Stories* (not included in the author's collections listed above)

"Mrs. Manstey's View." *Scribner's Magazine* 10, July, 1891, pp. 117–22.

"The Fulness of Life." *Scribner's Magazine* 14, December, 1893, pp. 699–704.

"That Good May Come." *Scribner's Magazine* 15, May, 1894, pp. 629–42.

"The Lamp of Psyche." *Scribner's Magazine* 18, October, 1895, pp. 418–28.

"The Valley of Childish Things and Other Emblems." *Century* 52, July, 1896, pp. 467–69.

"April Showers." *Youth's Companion* 74, January 18, 1900, pp. 25–26.

"Friends." *Youth's Companion* 74, August 23, 1900, pp. 405–406; August 30, 1900, pp. 417–18.

"The Line of Least Resistance." *Lippincott's Magazine* 66, October, 1900, pp. 559–70.

"The Letter." *Harper's Magazine* 108, April, 1904, pp. 781–89. Appears in the English edition of *The Descent of Man*.

"The House of the Dead Hand." *Atlantic Monthly* 94, August, 1904, pp. 145–60.

"The Introducers." *Ainslee's* 16, December, 1905, pp. 139–48; January, 1906, pp. 61–67.

"Les Metteurs en scène." *Revue des Deux Mondes* 47, 1908, pp. 692–708.

"Writing a War Story." *Woman's Home Companion* 46, September, 1919, pp. 17–19.

"In a Day." *Woman's Home Companion* 60, January, 1933, pp. 7–8, 46; February, 1933, pp. 15–16, 104, 106, 118.

4. *Reviews and Articles* (uncollected)

"More Love Letters of an Englishwoman." *Bookman* 12, February, 1901, pp. 562–63.

Edwin H. and Evangeline W. Blashfield, *Italian Cities. Bookman* 13, August, 1901, pp. 563–64.

Stephen Phillips, *Ulysses. Bookman* 15, April, 1902, pp. 168–70.

Review of Mrs. Fiske's performance in Lorimer Stoddard's dramatization of Hardy's *Tess of the D'Urbervilles*, New York *Commercial Advertiser*, May 7, 1902.

Leslie Stephen, *George Eliot. Bookman* 15, May, 1902, pp. 247–51.

"The Three Francescas." *North American Review* 175, July, 1902, pp. 17–30.

"The Vice of Reading." *North American Review* 177, October, 1903, pp. 513–21.

Howard Sturgis, *Belchamber. Bookman* 21, May, 1905, pp. 307–10.

Maurice Hewlett, *The Fool Errant. Bookman* 22, September, 1905, pp. 64–67.

Eugene Lee-Hamilton, *The Sonnets of the Wingless Hours. Bookman* 26, November, 1907, pp. 251–53.

"George Cabot Lodge." *Scribner's Magazine* 47, February, 1910, pp. 236–39.

"The Criticism of Fiction." *Times* Literary Supplement, May 14, 1914, pp. 229–30.

"Jean du Breuil de Saint-Germain." *Revue Hebdomadaire* 24, May 15, 1915, pp. 351–61.

"Les Français vus par une américaine." *Revue Hebdomadaire* 27, January 5, 1918, pp. 5–21.

"L'Amérique en guerre." *Revue Hebdomadaire* 27, March 2, 1918, pp. 5–28.

"How Paris Welcomed the King." *Réveillé*, no. 3, February, 1919, pp. 367–69.

"Henry James in His Letters." *Quarterly Review* 234, July, 1920, pp. 188–202.

"Christmas Tinsel." *Delineator* 103, December, 1923, p. 11.

"The Great American Novel." *Yale Review*, n.s. 16, July, 1927, pp. 646–56.

"William C. Brownell." *Scribner's Magazine* 84, November, 1928, pp. 596–602.

"A Cycle of Reviewing." *Spectator* (London) 141, November 23, 1928, supplement, p. 44.

"Visibility in Fiction." *Yale Review*, n.s. 18, March, 1929, pp. 480–88.

"Confessions of a Novelist." *Atlantic Monthly* 151, April, 1933, pp. 385–92.

"Tendencies in Modern Fiction." *Saturday Review of Literature* 10, January 27, 1934, pp. 433–44.

"Permanent Values in Fiction." *Saturday Review of Literature* 10, April 7, 1934, pp. 603–604.

"A Reconsideration of Proust." *Saturday Review of Literature* 11, October 27, 1934, pp. 233–34.

"Souvenirs du Bourget d'Outremer." *Revue Hebdomadaire* 45, June 21, 1936, pp. 266–86.

"A Little Girl's New York." *Harper's Magazine* 176, March, 1938, pp. 356–64.

5. *Prefaces and Introductions*

A Village Romeo and Juliet (Romeo und Julia auf dem Dorfe). By Gottfried Keller. Translated by Anna C. Bahlmann. Introduction by Edith Wharton. New York: Scribner's, 1914.

Futility. By William Gerhardi. Preface by Edith Wharton. New York: Duffield, 1922.

Benediction (Bénédiction). By Claude Silve (Comtesse Philomène de La Forest-Divonne). Translated by Robert Norton. Foreword by Edith Wharton. New York: Appleton-Century, 1936.

Ethan Frome. A dramatization of Edith Wharton's novel by Owen and Donald Davis. Foreword by Edith Wharton. New York: Scribner's, 1936.

II. WORKS ABOUT EDITH WHARTON

Anderson, Hilton. "Edith Wharton and the Vulgar American." *Southern Quarterly* 7, October, 1968, pp. 17–22.

———. "Edith Wharton as a Fictional Heroine." *South Atlantic Quarterly* 69, Winter, 1970, pp. 118–23.

Auchincloss, Louis. *Edith Wharton.* Minneapolis: University of Minnesota Press, 1961. Appears also in *Seven Modern Ameri-*

can Novelists, edited by William Van O'Connor. Minneapolis: University of Minnesota Press, 1964.

> She wanted nothing less than to interpret the age in which she
> lived and to seek out the origin and cause of the increasing num-
> ber of things that angered her.

———. *Edith Wharton: A Woman in Her Time*. New York:
Viking Press, 1971.

———. "Edith Wharton and Her New Yorks." *Partisan Review*
18, July-August, 1951, pp. 411–19. Appears also in *Reflections of a Jacobite*. Boston: Houghton Mifflin, 1961.

Bell, Millicent. *Edith Wharton and Henry James: The Story of
Their Friendship*. New York: Braziller, 1965.

Bernard, Kenneth. "Imagery and Symbolism in *Ethan Frome*."
College English 23, December, 1961, pp. 178–84.

Bourget, Paul. Introduction to *Chez les heureux du monde* (*The
House of Mirth*), translated by Charles Du Bos. Paris: Plon-
Nourrit, 1908.

Brennan, Joseph X. "*Ethan Frome:* Structure and Metaphor."
Modern Fiction Studies 7, Winter, 1961–62, pp. 347–56.

Brenni, Vito J. *Edith Wharton: A Bibliography*. Morgantown:
West Virginia University Library, 1966.

Brooks, Van Wyck. *The Confident Years*. New York: Dutton,
1952. Pp. 283–300.

> The circumstances that shaped her mind were much like those
> of Henry James . . . for, however much she was in America, she
> was of it only in a sense and Europe was a larger fact in .her
> imagination.

Brown, E. K. *Edith Wharton: Étude critique*. Paris: Librairie E.
Droz, 1935.

Carroll, Loren. "Edith Wharton in Profile." *The Herald Tribune*,
European edition, November 16, 1936.

Clough, David. "Edith Wharton's War Novels: A Reappraisal."
Twentieth Century Literature 19, January, 1973, pp. 1–14.

Coolidge, Olivia. *Edith Wharton, 1862–1937*. New York: Scribner's, 1964.

Extracts from selected critical works about Wharton in the
critics' own words have been included.—AU.

Cross, Wilbur L. "Edith Wharton." *Bookman* 63, August, 1926, pp. 641–46.

Davis, Lavinia R. *A Bibliography of the Writings of Edith Wharton*. Portland, Maine: Southwood Press, 1933.

Gargano, James W. "*The House of Mirth:* Social Futility and Faith." *American Literature* 44, March, 1972, pp. 137–43.

Gerould, Katharine Fullerton. *Edith Wharton: A Critical Study*. New York: Appleton, n.d.

Grant, Robert. *Commemorative Tributes to E. A. Robinson and Others*. New York: Publications of the American Academy of Arts and Letters (no. 95), 1939. Pp. 43–59.

Herrick, Robert. "Mrs. Wharton's World." *New Republic* 2, February 13, 1915, pp. 40–42.

Hoffman, Frederick J. *The Modern Novel in America: 1900–1950*. Chicago: Regnery, 1951. Pp. 11–20.

———. "Points of Moral Reference: A Comparative Study of Edith Wharton and F. Scott Fitzgerald," in *English Institute Essays*, 1949. New York: Columbia University Press, 1950. Pp. 147–76.

Hopkins, Viola. "The Ordering Style in *The Age of Innocence*." *American Literature* 30, November, 1958, pp. 345–57.

Howe, Irving. "Introduction: The Achievement of Edith Wharton," in *Edith Wharton: A Collection of Critical Essays*, edited by Irving Howe. Englewood Cliffs, N.J.: Prentice-Hall, 1962.

> In Mrs. Wharton's vision of things—and we can only speculate on the extent to which her personal unhappiness contributed to it—human beings seem always to prove inadequate, always to fail each other, always to be the victims of an innate disharmony between love and response, need and capacity.

James, Henry. *The Letters of Henry James*, edited by Percy Lubbock. New York: Scribner's, 1920. Vol. II, pp. 281–85. Analysis of *The Reef*.

———. *Notes on Novelists, with Some Other Notes*. New York: Scribner's, 1914. Pp. 353–56. Estimate of *The Custom of the Country*.

Kazin, Alfred. *On Native Grounds*. New York: Reynal & Hitchcock, 1942. Pp. 73–82.

> To Edith Wharton, whose very career as a novelist was the
> tenuous product of so many personal maladjustments, the novel
> became an involuted expression of self.

Kellogg, Grace. *The Two Lives of Edith Wharton.* New York:
Appleton-Century-Crofts, 1965.

Küster, Dieter. *Das Frankreichbild im Werk Edith Whartons.*
Bern: Herbert Lang, 1972.

LaGuardia, Eric. "Edith Wharton on Critics and Criticism."
Modern Language Notes 73, December, 1958, pp. 587–89.

Lawson, Richard H. *Edith Wharton and German Literature.*
Bonn: Bouvier Verlag Herbert Grundmann, 1974.

————. "Gesellschaft als Verbindungselement zwischen den
Seldwyla-Novellen Gottfried Kellers und den Romanen
Edith Whartons," in *Sprache, Dichtung, Gesellschaft*, edited
by Victor Lange and Hans-Gert Roloff. Frankfurt am Main:
Athenäum, 1971. Pp. 265–71.

————. "Hermann Sudermann and Edith Wharton." *Revue de
Littérature Comparée* 41, January-March, 1967, pp. 125–31.

————. "The Influence of Gottfried Keller on Edith Wharton."
Revue de Littérature Comparée 42, July-September, 1968,
pp. 366–79.

Leavis, Q. D. "Henry James's Heiress: The Importance of Edith
Wharton." *Scrutiny* 7, December, 1938, pp. 261–76.

> She was also an extraordinarily acute and far-sighted social critic;
> in this she was original and appears far more so when we think
> with what an effort this detachment must have been achieved by
> the child brought up to believe it her ambition to become, like
> her mother, the best-dressed woman in New York. . . .

Lewis, R. W. B. *Edith Wharton: A Biography.* New York:
Harper and Row, 1975.

Lindberg, Gary H. *Edith Wharton and the Novel of Manners.*
Charlottesville: University Press of Virginia, 1975.

Lovett, Robert M. *Edith Wharton.* New York: McBride, 1925.

Lubbock, Percy. "The Novels of Edith Wharton." *Quarterly
Review* 224, January, 1915, pp. 182–201.

> Mrs. Wharton's books, from the earliest to the latest, are more
> than a collection of penetrating and finely finished studies; they
> are linked episodes in one continuous adventure, the adventure
> of her rare and distinguished critical intelligence.

————. *Portrait of Edith Wharton.* New York: Appleton-Century, 1947.

Lyde, Marilyn Jones. *Edith Wharton: Convention and Morality in the Work of a Novelist.* Norman: University of Oklahoma Press, 1959.

Mansfield, Katherine. *Novels and Novelists,* edited by J. M. Murry. New York: Knopf, 1930. Pp. 316–20. On *The Age of Innocence.*

> To evoke the 1870s is to evoke irony and romance at once, and to keep the two balanced by all manner of delicate adjustments is so much a matter for her skillful hand that it seems more like play than work.

McDowell, Margaret B. *Edith Wharton.* Boston: Twayne, 1976.

————. "Edith Wharton's Ghost Stories." *Criticism* 12, Spring, 1970, pp. 132–52.

————. "Viewing the Custom of her Country: Edith Wharton's Feminism." *Contemporary Literature* 15, Autumn, 1974, pp. 521–38.

McHaney, Thomas L. "Fouqué's *Undine* and Edith Wharton's *Custom of the Country.*" *Revue de Littérature Comparée* 45, January-March, 1971, pp. 80–86.

McManis, Jo Agnew. "Edith Wharton's Hymns to Respectability." *Southern Review,* n.s. 7, October, 1971, pp. 986–93.

Michaud, Régis. *Le Roman américain d'aujourd'hui.* Paris: Boivin, 1926. Pp. 39–46, 55–79.

Moseley, Edwin M. "*The Age of Innocence:* Edith Wharton's Weak Faust." *College English* 21, December, 1959, pp. 156–60.

Nevius, Blake. *Edith Wharton.* Berkeley and Los Angeles: University of California Press, 1953.

Niall, Brenda. "Prufrock in Brownstone: Edith Wharton's *The Age of Innocence.*" *Southern Review* (Australia) 4, November, 1971, pp. 203–14.

Plante, Patricia R. "Edith Wharton and the Invading Goths." *Midcontinent American Studies Journal* 5, Fall, 1964, pp. 18–23.

Puknat, E. M. and S. B. "Edith Wharton and Gottfried Keller." *Comparative Literature* 21, Summer, 1969, pp. 245–54.

Sencourt, Robert. "The Poetry of Edith Wharton." *Bookman*
    73, July, 1931, pp. 478–86.

Trilling, Diana. "The House of Mirth Revisited." *Harper's
    Bazaar* 81, December, 1947, pp. 126–27, 181–86.

> *The House of Mirth* is nevertheless one of the most telling in-
> dictments of a social system based on the chance distribution of
> wealth, and therefore of social privilege, that has ever been put
> on paper.

Trueblood, Charles K. "Edith Wharton." *Dial* 68, January, 1920,
    pp. 80–91.

Tuttleton, James W. "Edith Wharton: Form and the Episte-
    mology of Literary Creation." *Criticism* 10, Fall, 1968, pp.
    334–51.

Underwood, John C. *Literature and Insurgency: Ten Studies in
    Racial Evolution*. New York: Mitchell Kennerley, 1914. Pp.
    346–90.

Waldstein, Charles. "Social Ideals." *North American Review*
    182, June, 1906, pp. 840–52; 183, July, 1906, pp. 125–36.

Walton, Geoffrey. *Edith Wharton: A Critical Interpretation*.
    Rutherford, N.J.: Fairleigh Dickinson University Press,
    1970.

Wegelin, Christof. "Edith Wharton and the Twilight of the
    International Novel." *Southern Review*, n.s. 5, April, 1969,
    pp. 398–418.

Wilson, Edmund. *Classics and Commercials*. New York: Farrar,
    Straus, 1950. Pp. 412–18.

———. *The Wound and the Bow*. Boston: Houghton Mifflin,
    1941. Pp. 195–213.

> Her tragic heroines and heroes are the victims of the group
> pressure of convention; they are passionate or imaginative spirits,
> hungry for emotional and intellectual experience, who find them-
> selves locked into a small closed system, and either destroy them-
> selves by beating their heads against their prison or suffer a living
> death in resigning themselves to it.

Winner, Viola Hopkins. "Convention and Prediction in Edith
    Wharton's *Fast and Loose*." *American Literature* 42, March,
    1970, pp. 50–69.

Wolff, Cynthia Griffin. "Lily Bart and the Beautiful Death."
    American Literature 46, March, 1974, pp. 16–40.

Index

MODERN LITERATURE MONOGRAPHS